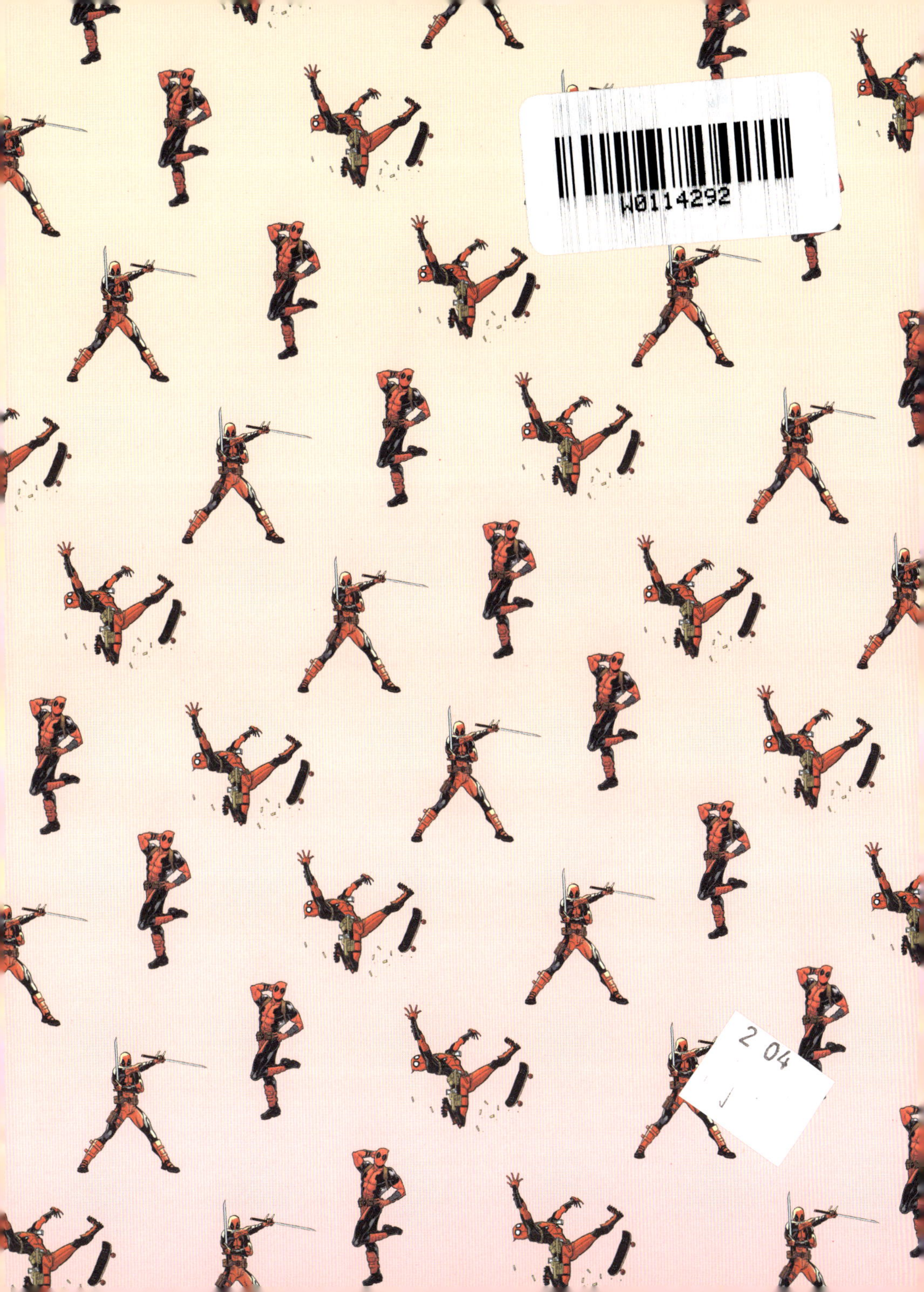

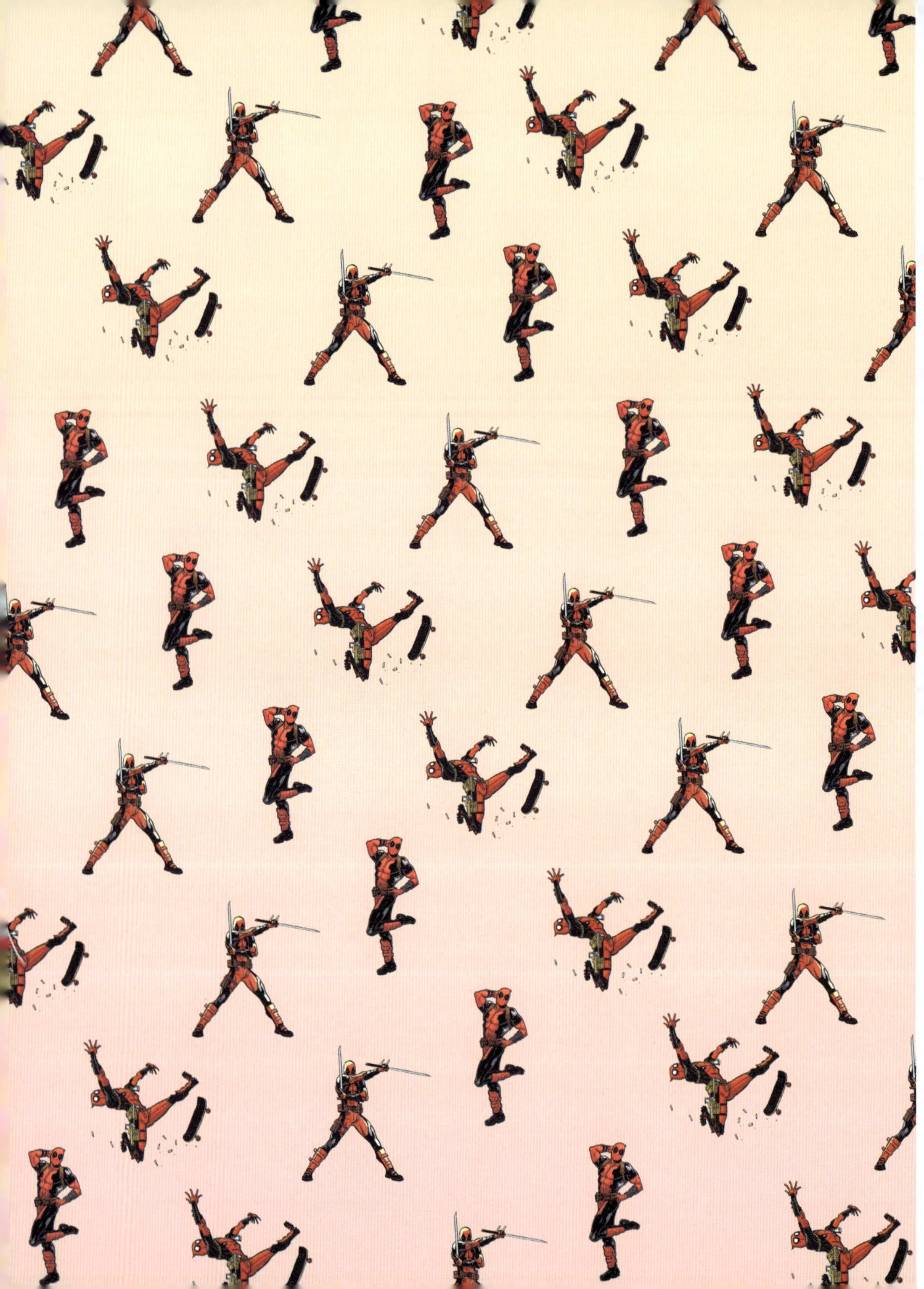

MARVEL

DEADPOOL's

Affirmations

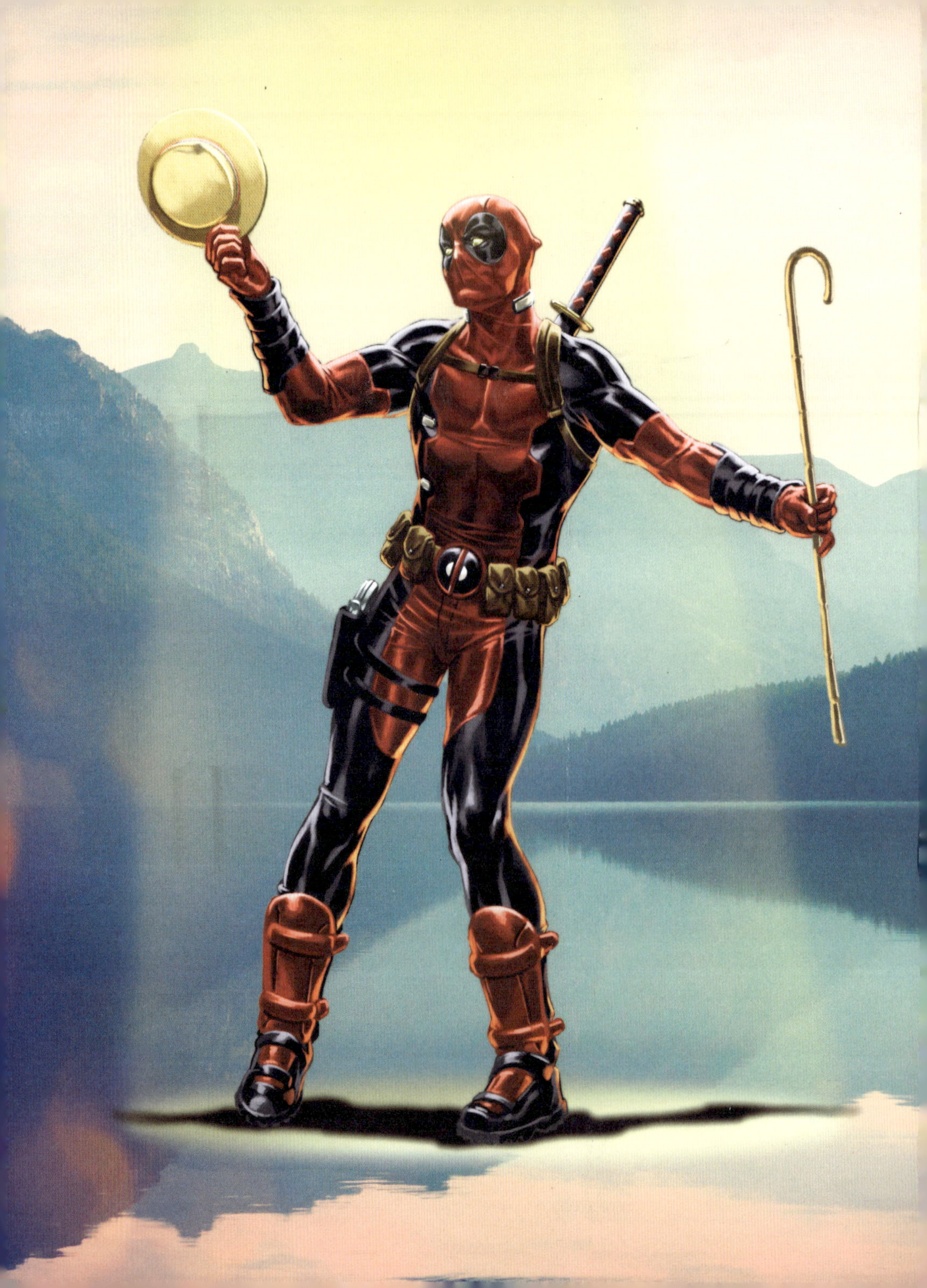

MARVEL

DEADPOOL's
Affirmations

Feel Yourself to Heal Yourself

Rob Kutner

RANDOM HOUSE WORLDS
NEW YORK

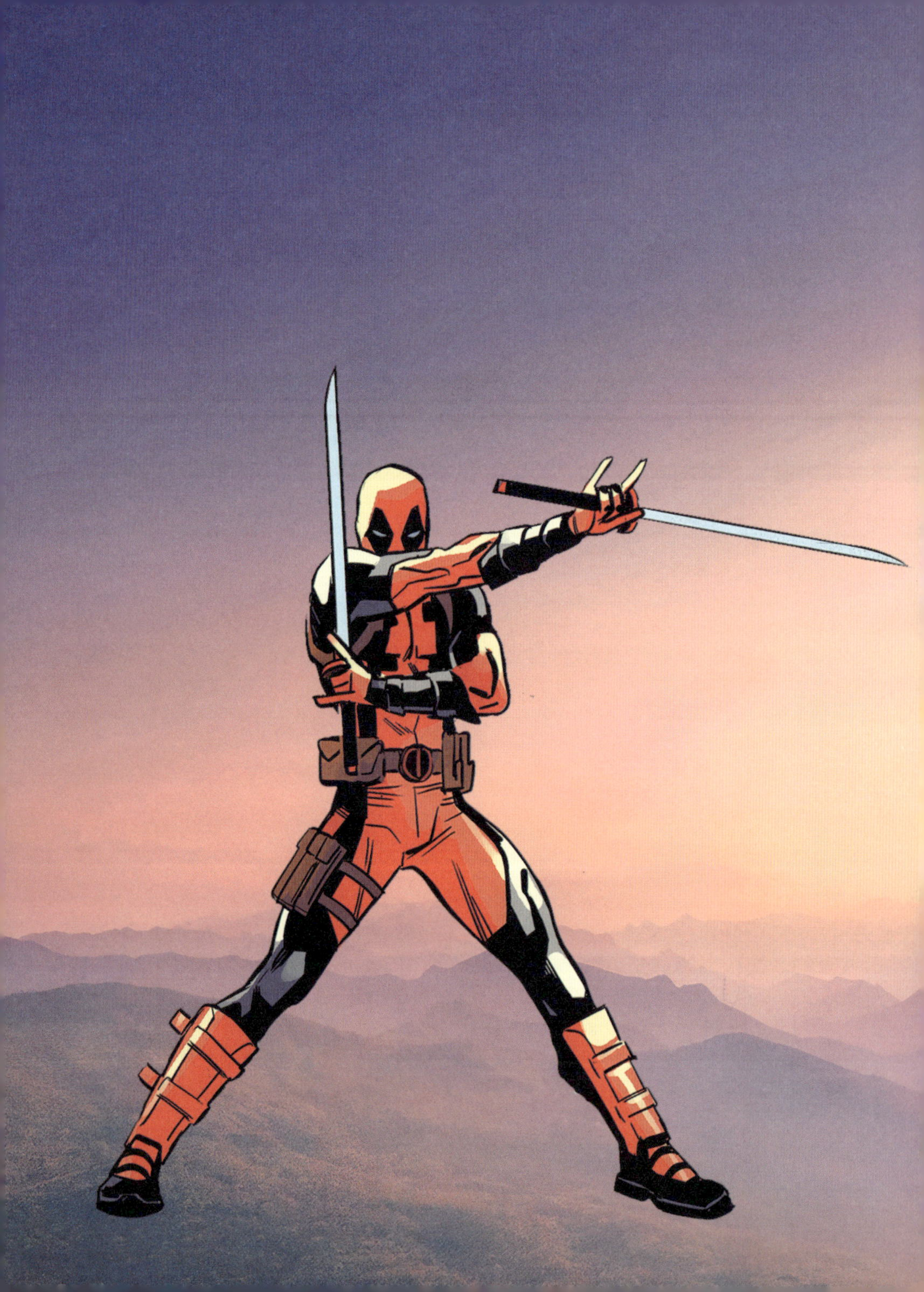

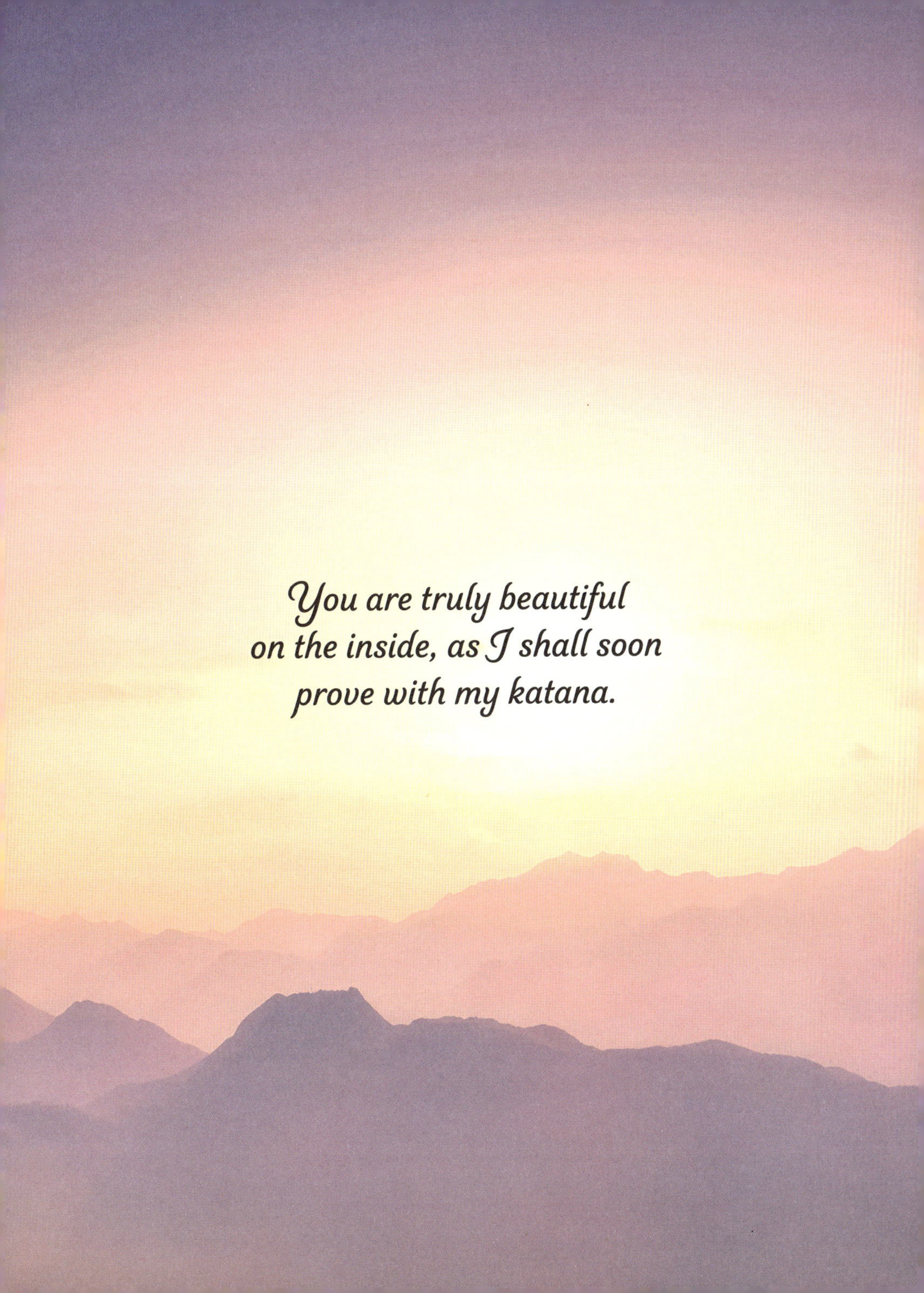

*You are truly beautiful
on the inside, as I shall soon
prove with my katana.*

Every day and in every way you
are getting better, not unlike the
stumps that used to be my second
through fourth left toes after
I called Wolverine "Sir Pointyhair."

ZONE OF
OUCHY

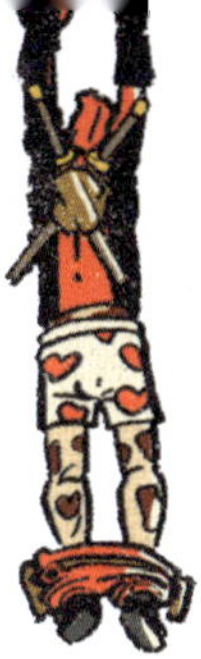

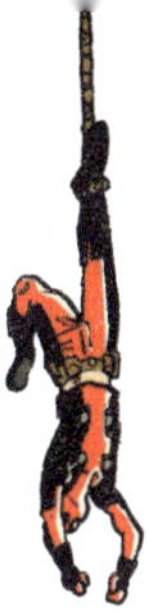

Don't let anyone put you in a box, *even* if they *claim* it will increase your collector's value. Ten thousand Li'l Plastic Mes are suffocating!

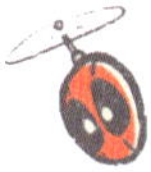

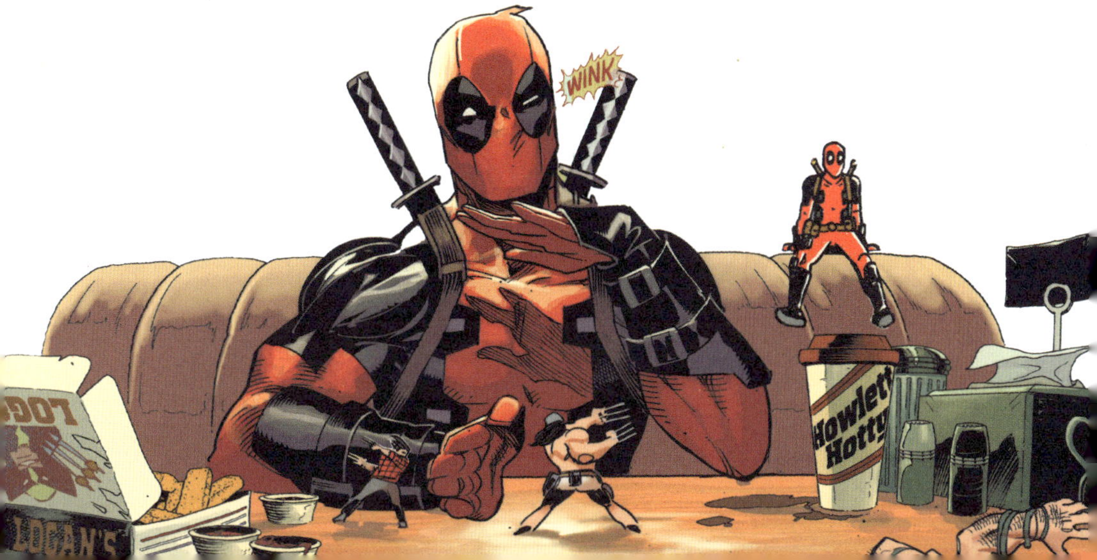
WINK
LOGAN'S

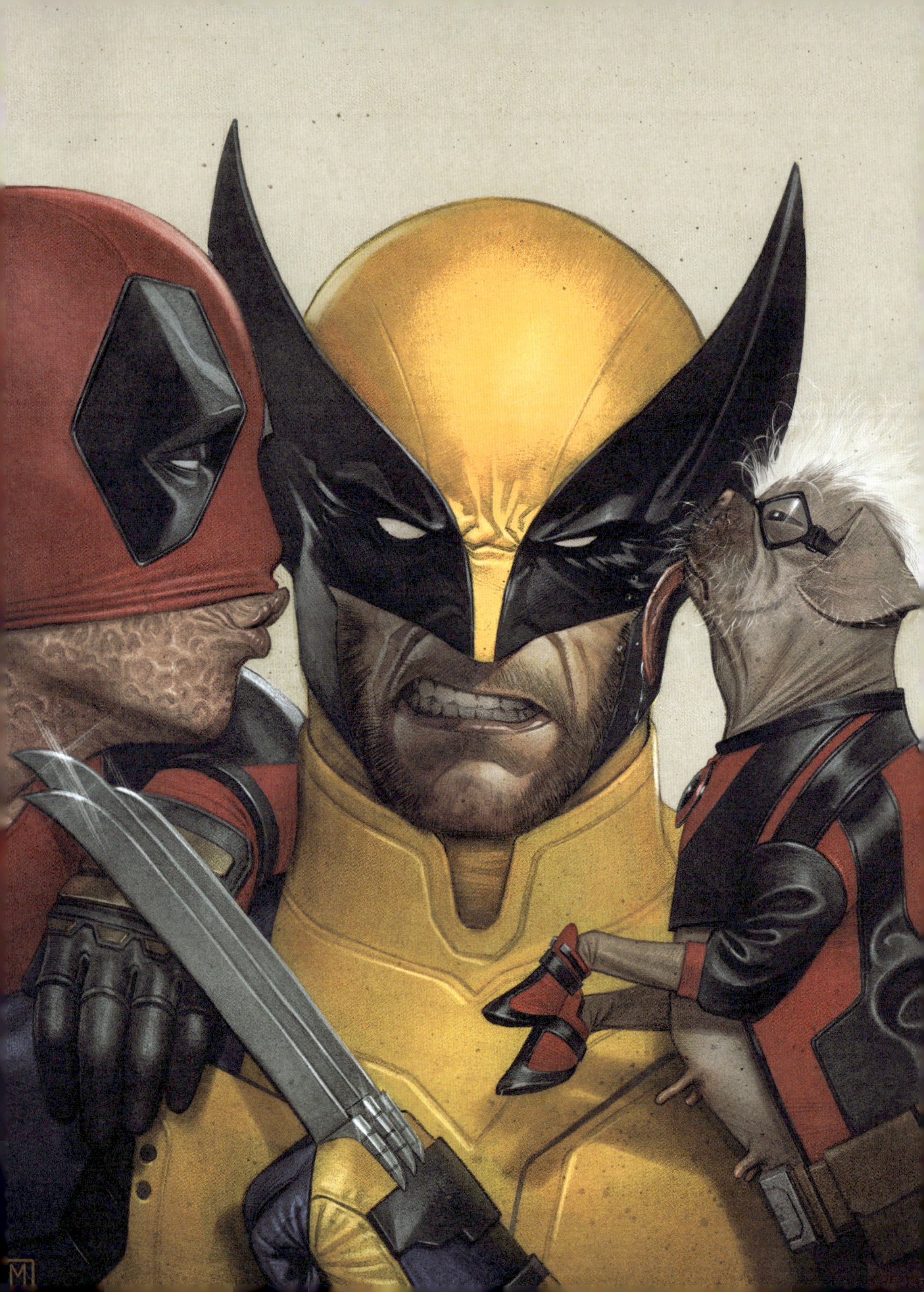

Never forget
that you have the power
to put a smile on
someone else's face.

Pro tip: Blood makes a
great lipstick, unless
they're an Autumn.

Today is the perfect day
to fall in love with yourself.
Tomorrow, third base.

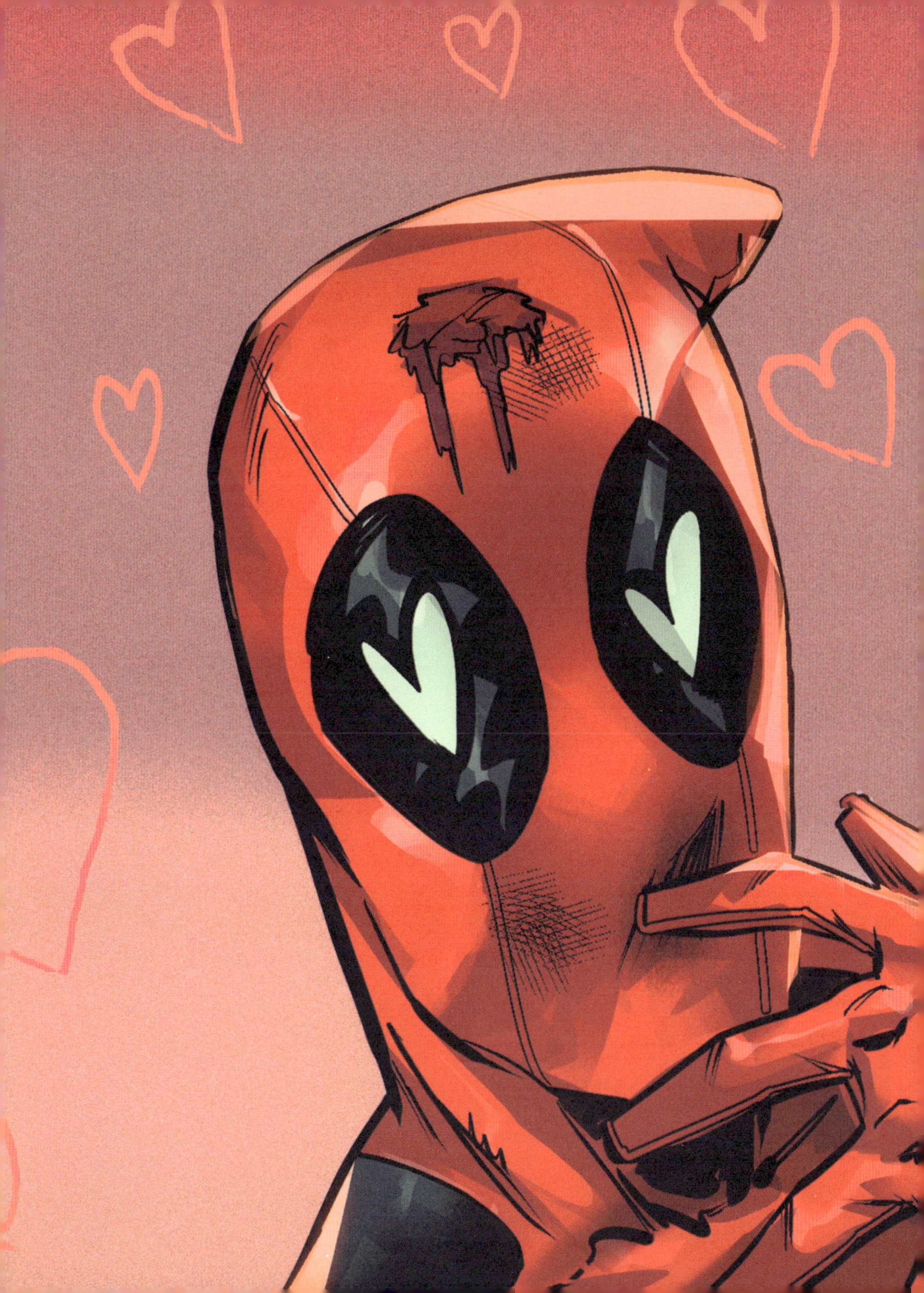

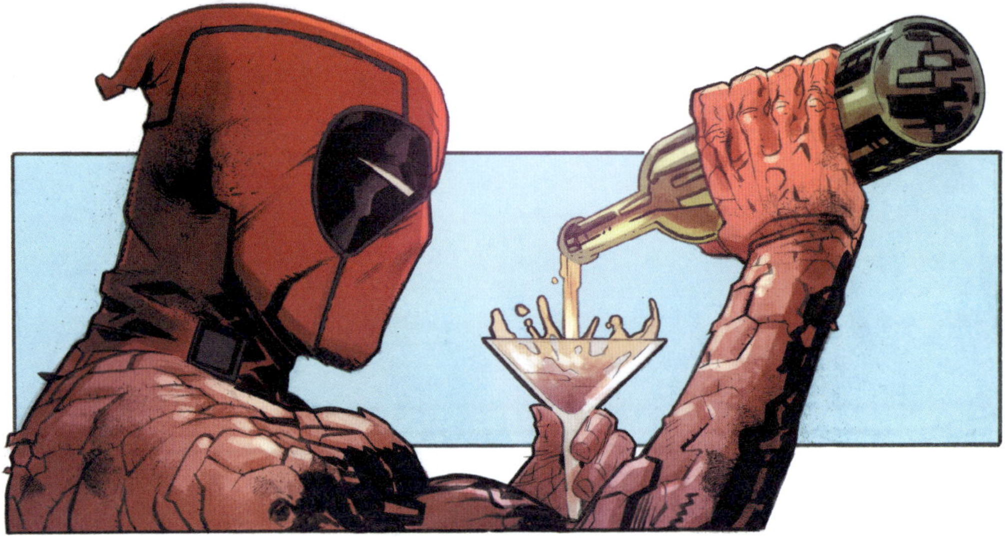

Make every day feel like your
birthday: Take a bath. Grow back
a body part. Even that one.
What the heck, it's your day!

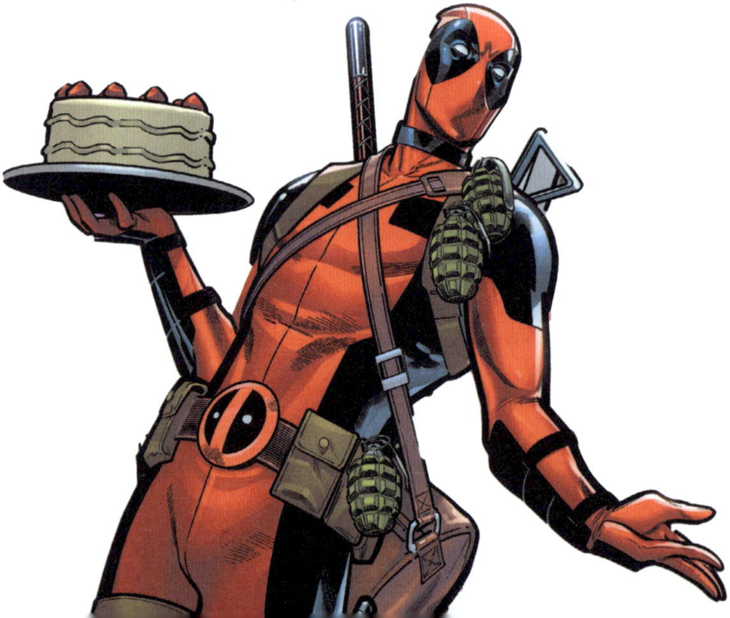

When the world
has got you down,
just remember
all the people you
can still kill from
the ground!

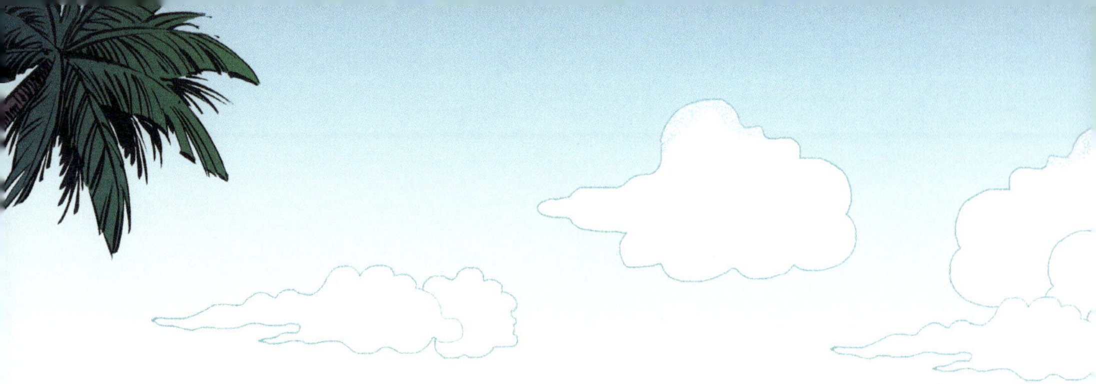

No matter what happens,
you are in the driver's seat

(and eventually they are
going to get your drive-thru
chimichanga order right).

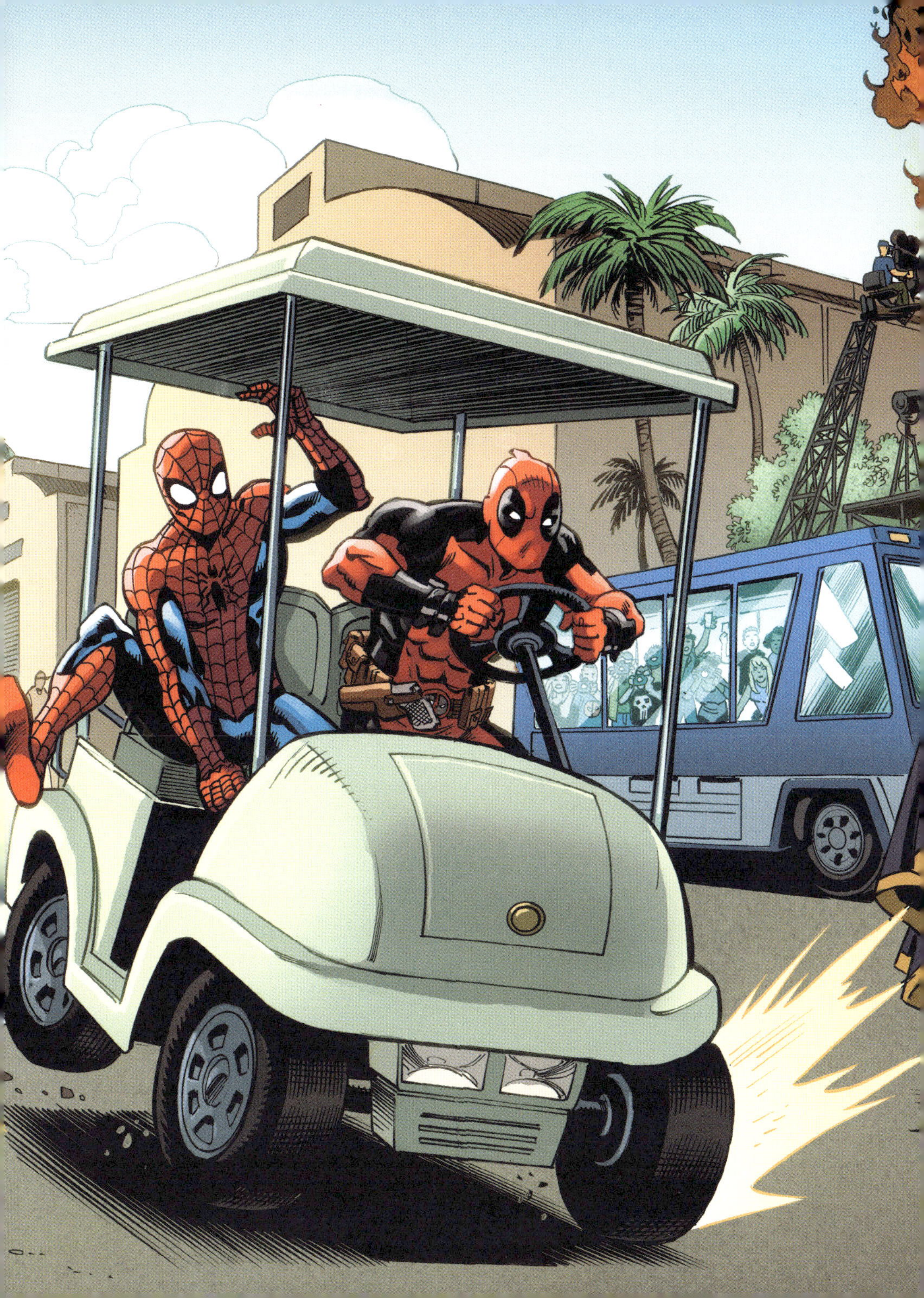

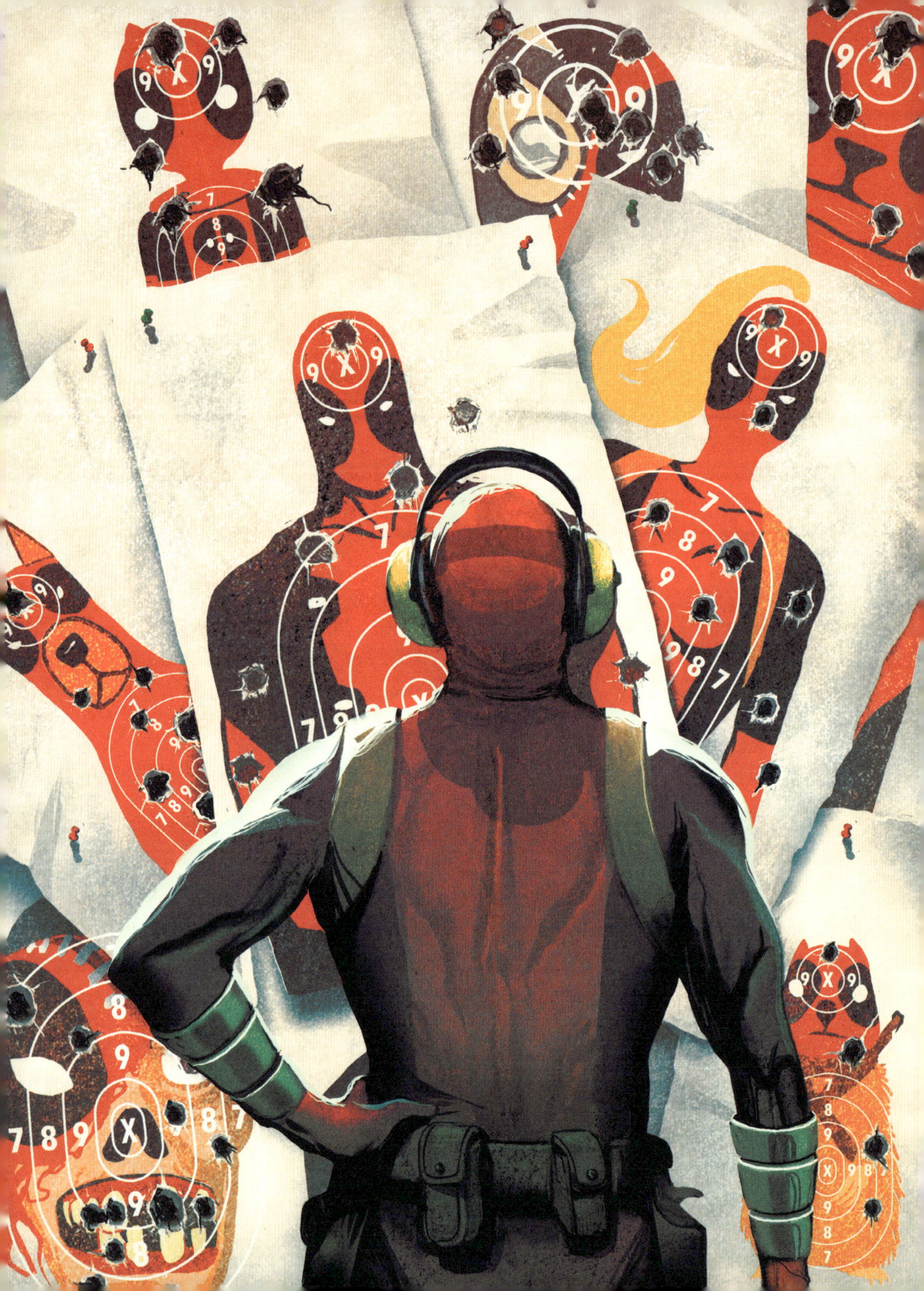

You are multidimensional.

Be kind to every version of yourself.

Relax, put your feet up,
and hey, if they get pulverized
by a spray of enemy gunfire,
you'll grow more. Chill.

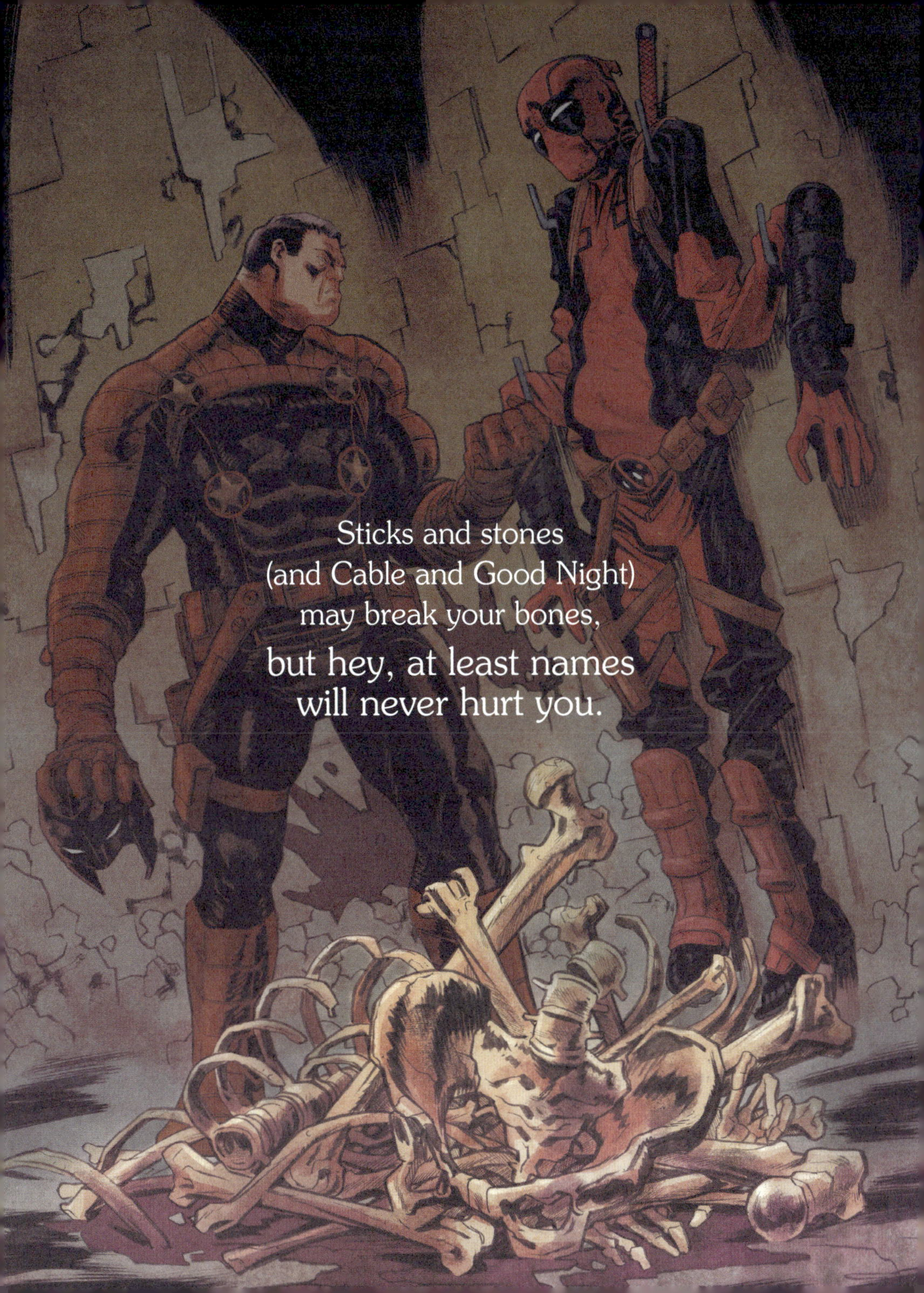
Sticks and stones
(and Cable and Good Night)
may break your bones,
but hey, at least names
will never hurt you.

Become your own superfan:
Throw a YouCon, sell You
merch to yourself, go so crazy
that You eventually have to
block your own cell number.

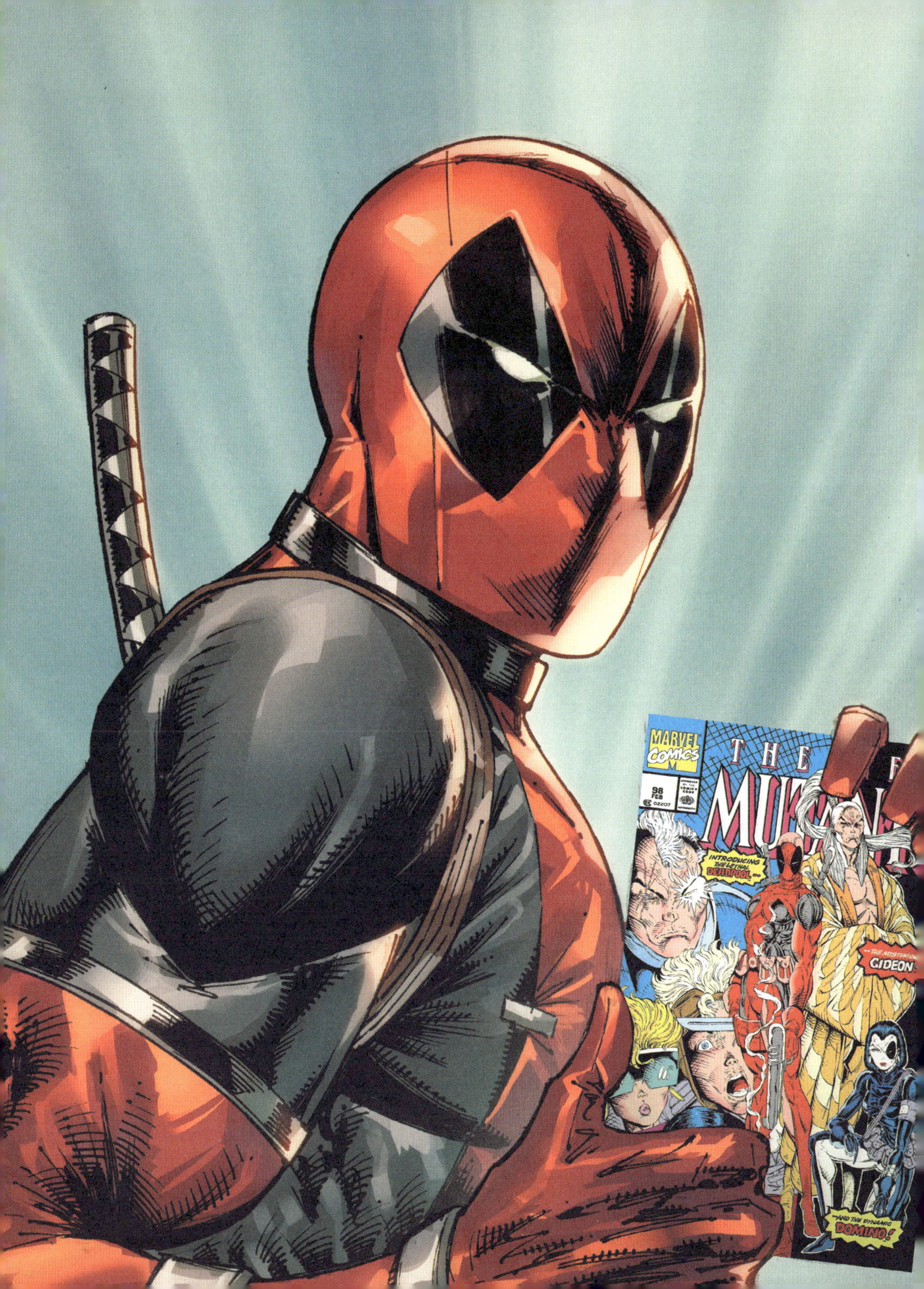
MARVEL COMICS
THE
98 FEB
INTRODUCING THE LETHAL DEADPOOL --
-- THE
GIDEON
--AND THE DYNAMIC DOMINO!

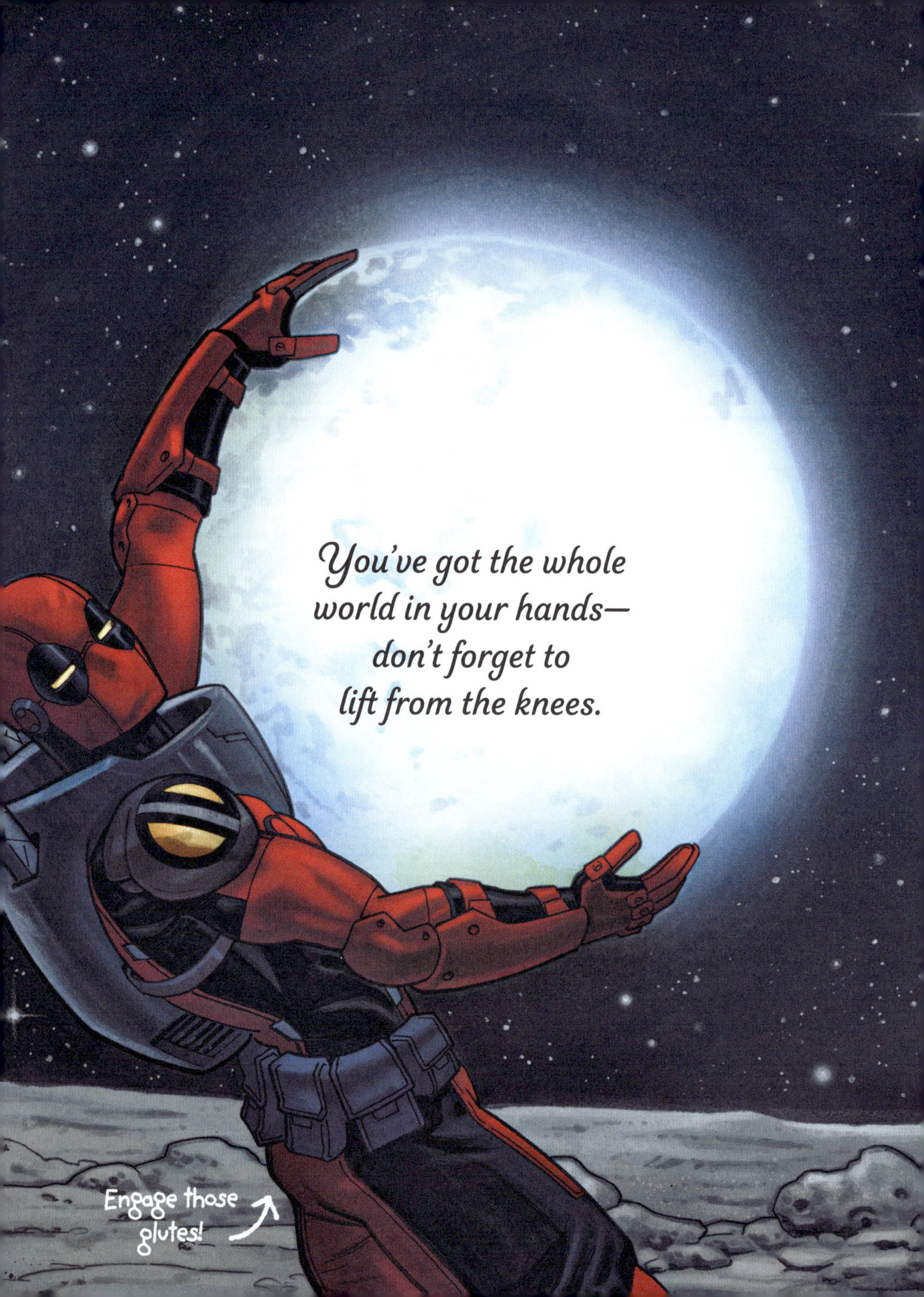
You've got the whole world in your hands— don't forget to lift from the knees.
Engage those glutes!

KEEP GETTING BACK UP,

just like me after
my twenty-seventh attempt
at a super hero landing!

Don't be afraid to cry.
Crying gets the hurt out...
not to mention that tears
taste delicious when dripped
all over fresh mango.
Follow me for more emotional
wellness/mango tips!

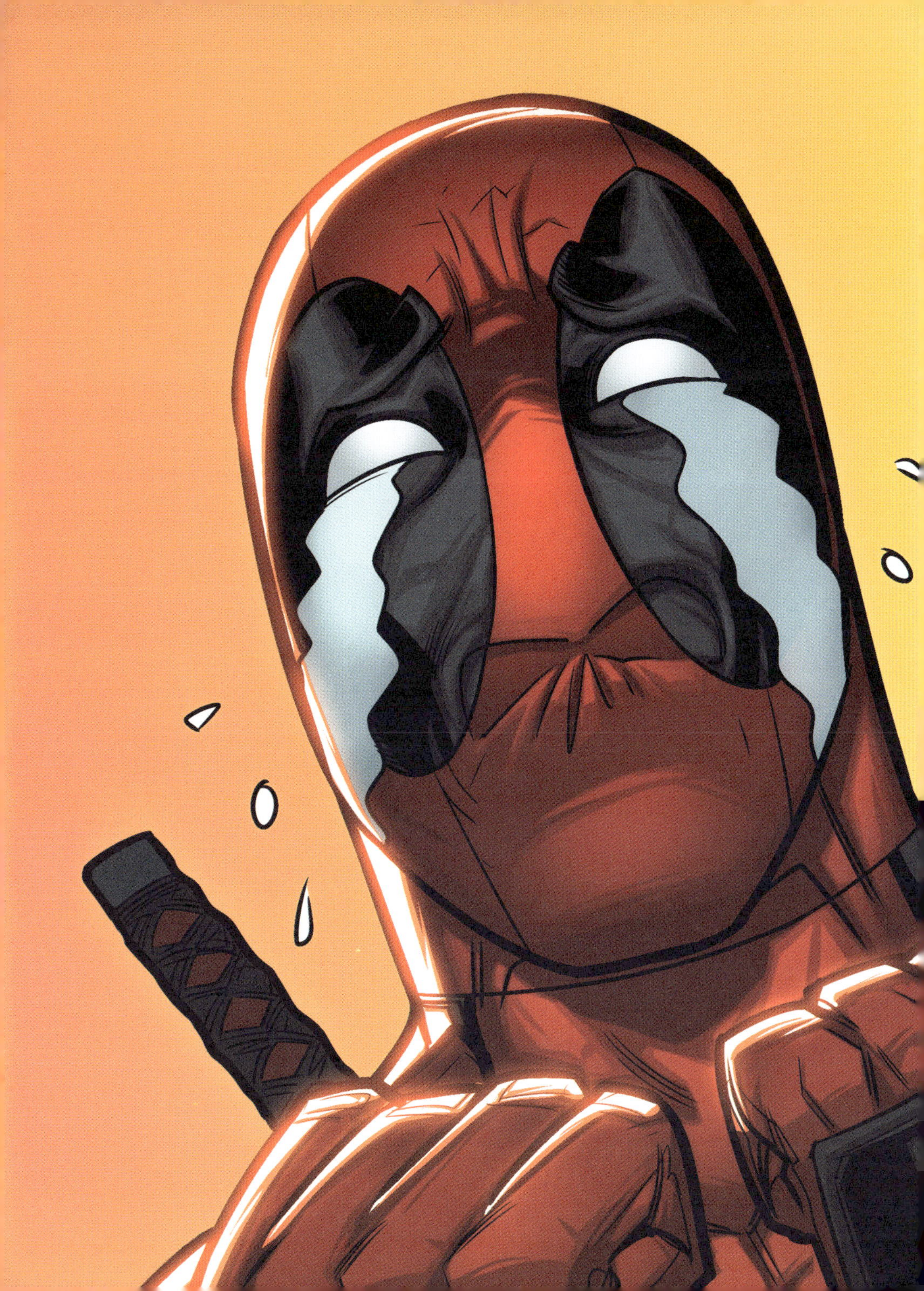

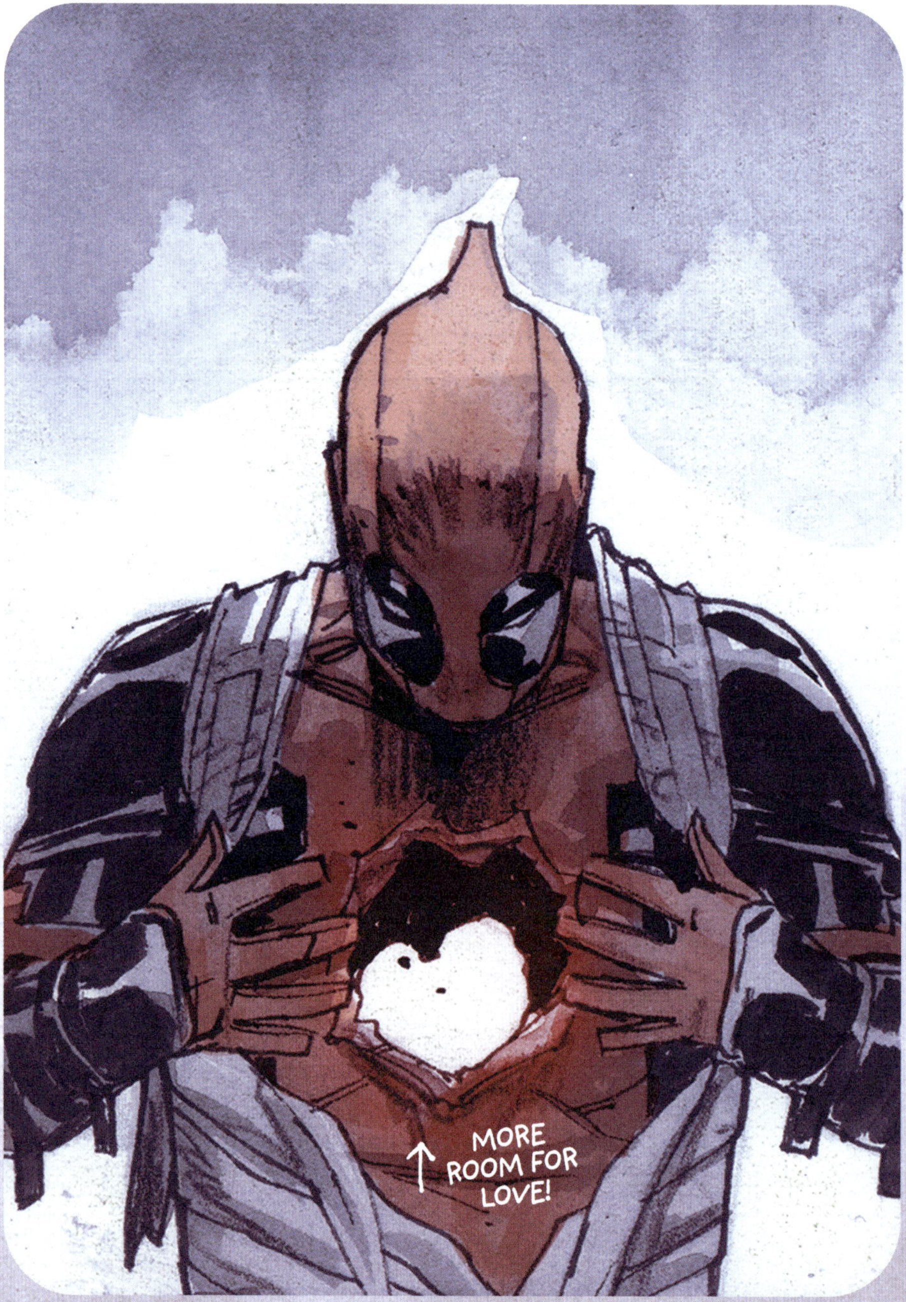
MORE ROOM FOR LOVE!

YOU are the master of
your own heart . . .

even on the days when you
wake up with a hole in your chest
where your heart used to be.

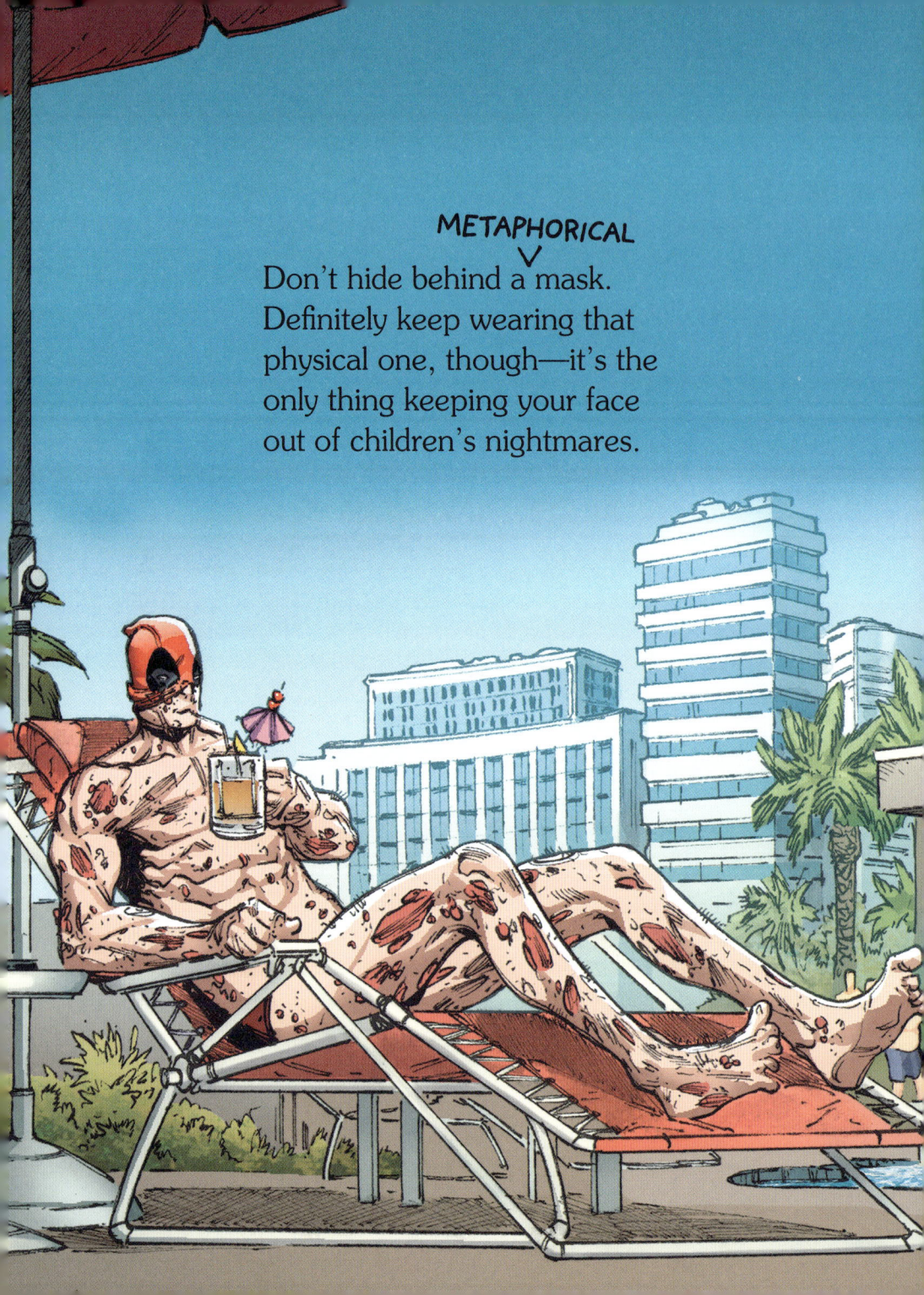

METAPHORICAL
∨
Don't hide behind a mask.
Definitely keep wearing that
physical one, though—it's the
only thing keeping your face
out of children's nightmares.

Don't be jealous of others
who are able to find joy;
steal their joy objects.

Life is too short for regrets,
and if you keep regretting,
I will make it even shorter.
Good talk!

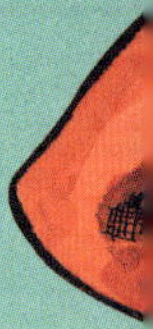

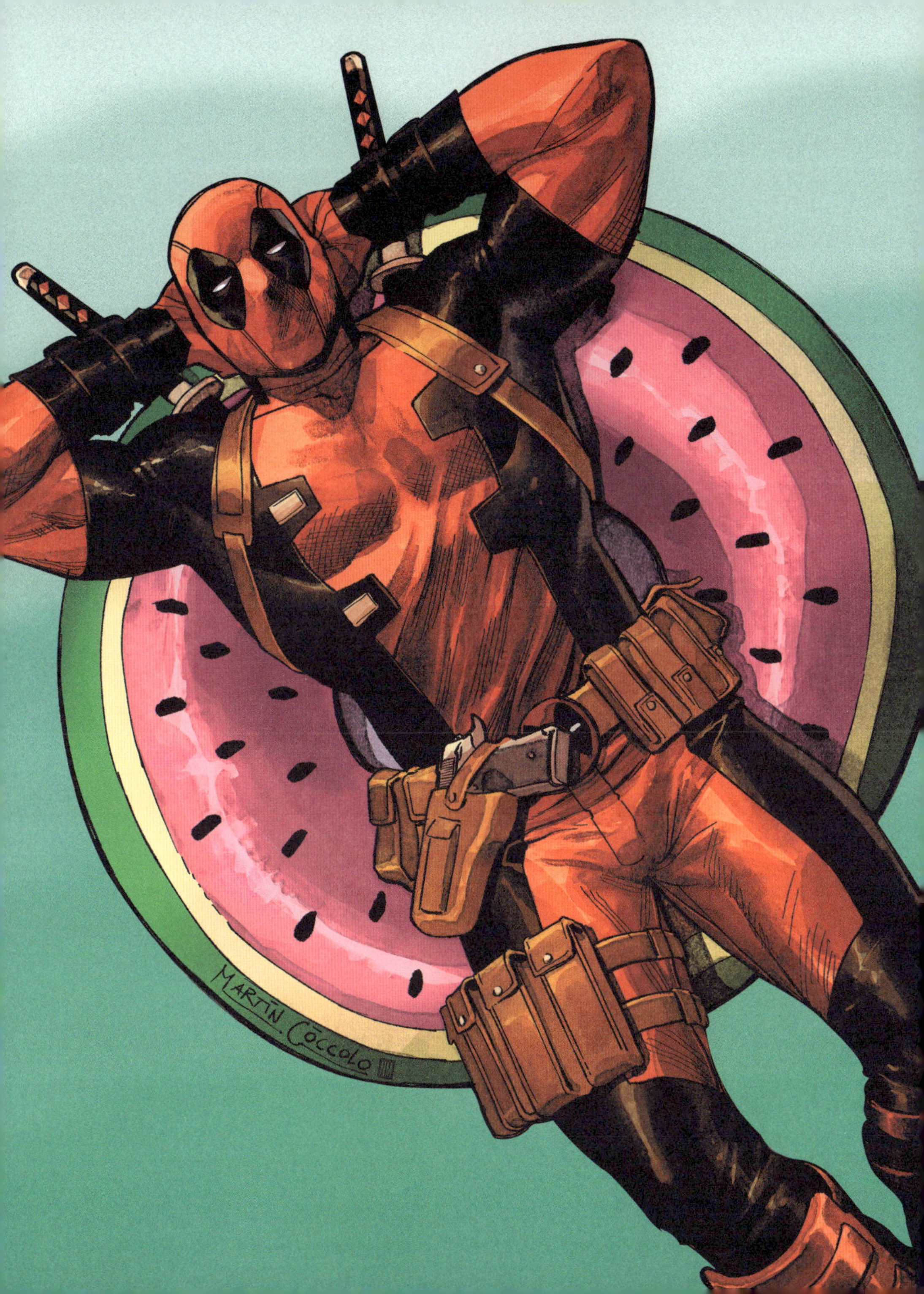
MARTIN COCCOLO

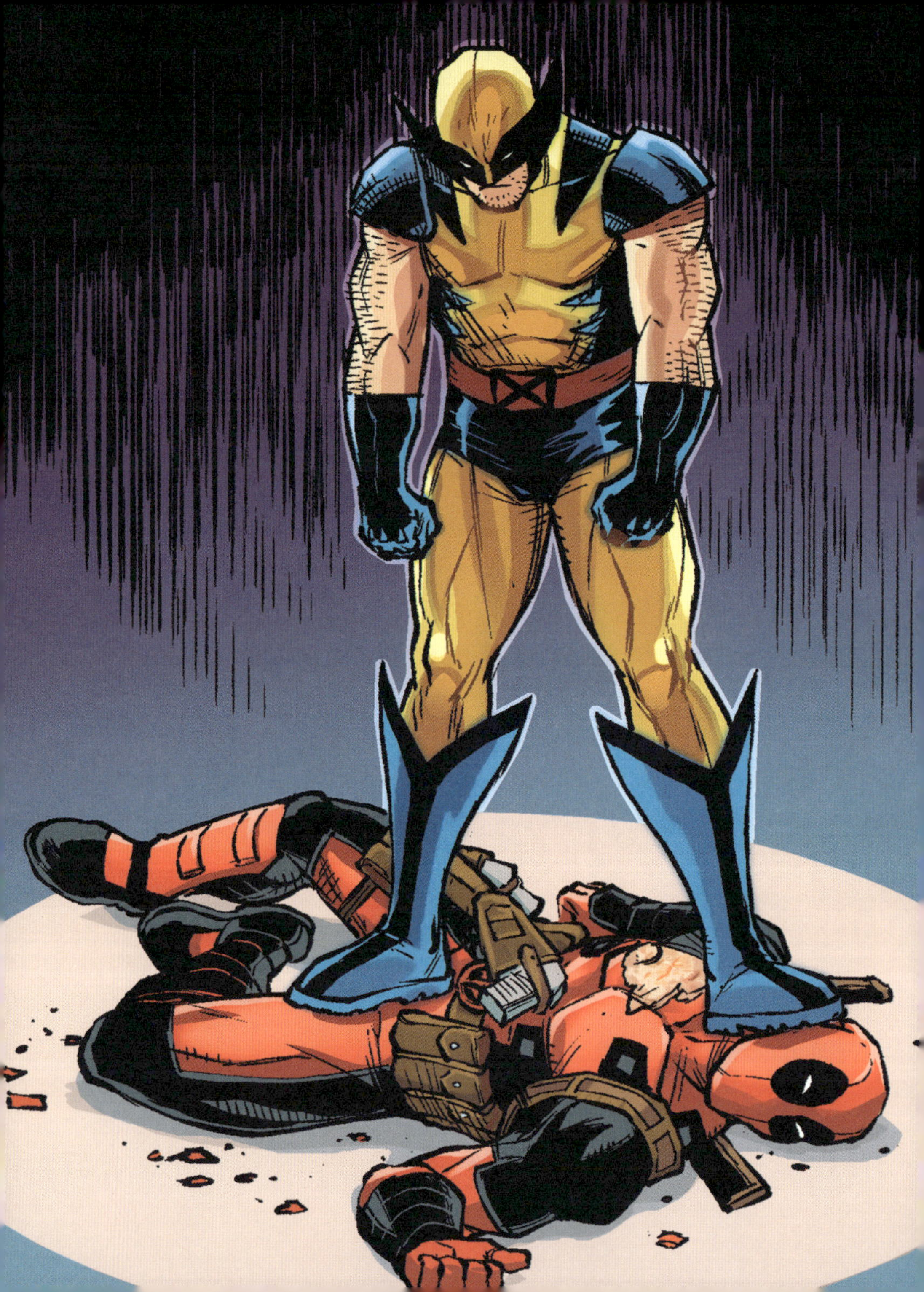

Stand up and speak loudly, because you've got something to say. No matter **WHAT** *kind of boot is currently crushing your mouth-bone.*

Don't be content
with being #1.

Raise **TWO** fingers
to the sky and proclaim
"I'm #1" with each finger,

which technically
makes you #2.

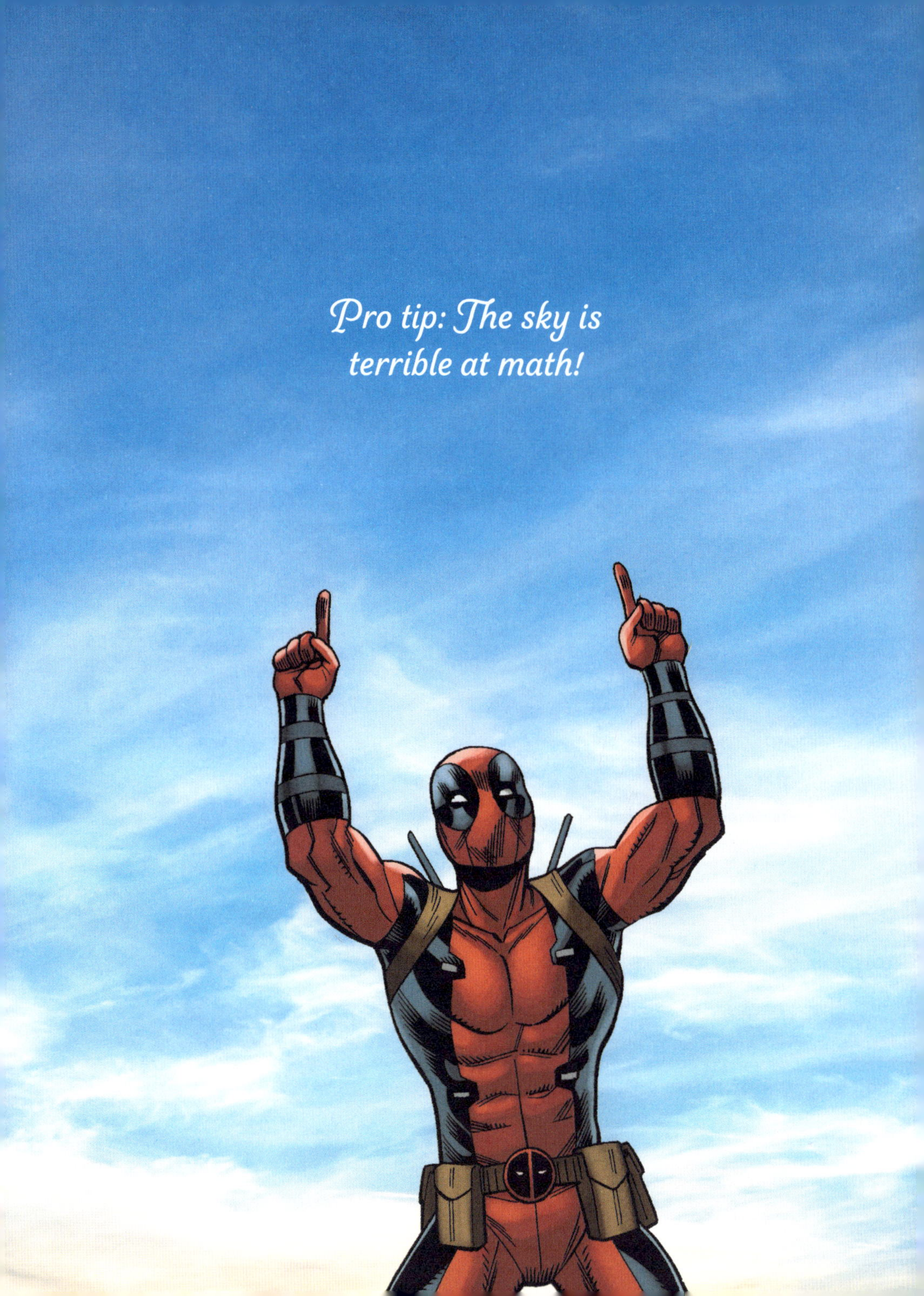
Pro tip: The sky is terrible at math!

Speak kindly to yourself,
and to Spidey.

Shower everyone
else with threats of violence.

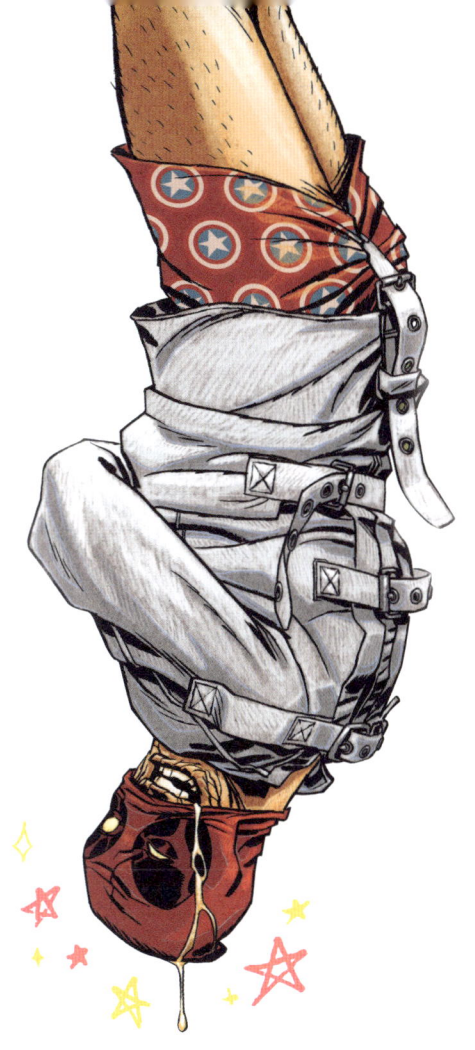

It's not you who's upside down,
it's the world that is!
And also, the world's head is
filling up with blood and
seeing cartoon stars, too, right?

Start each day by taking a good,
long look in the mirror . . .
because that's the easiest way to
spot the ninjas in demon masks
lurking behind you.
Nice try, Ninjy!

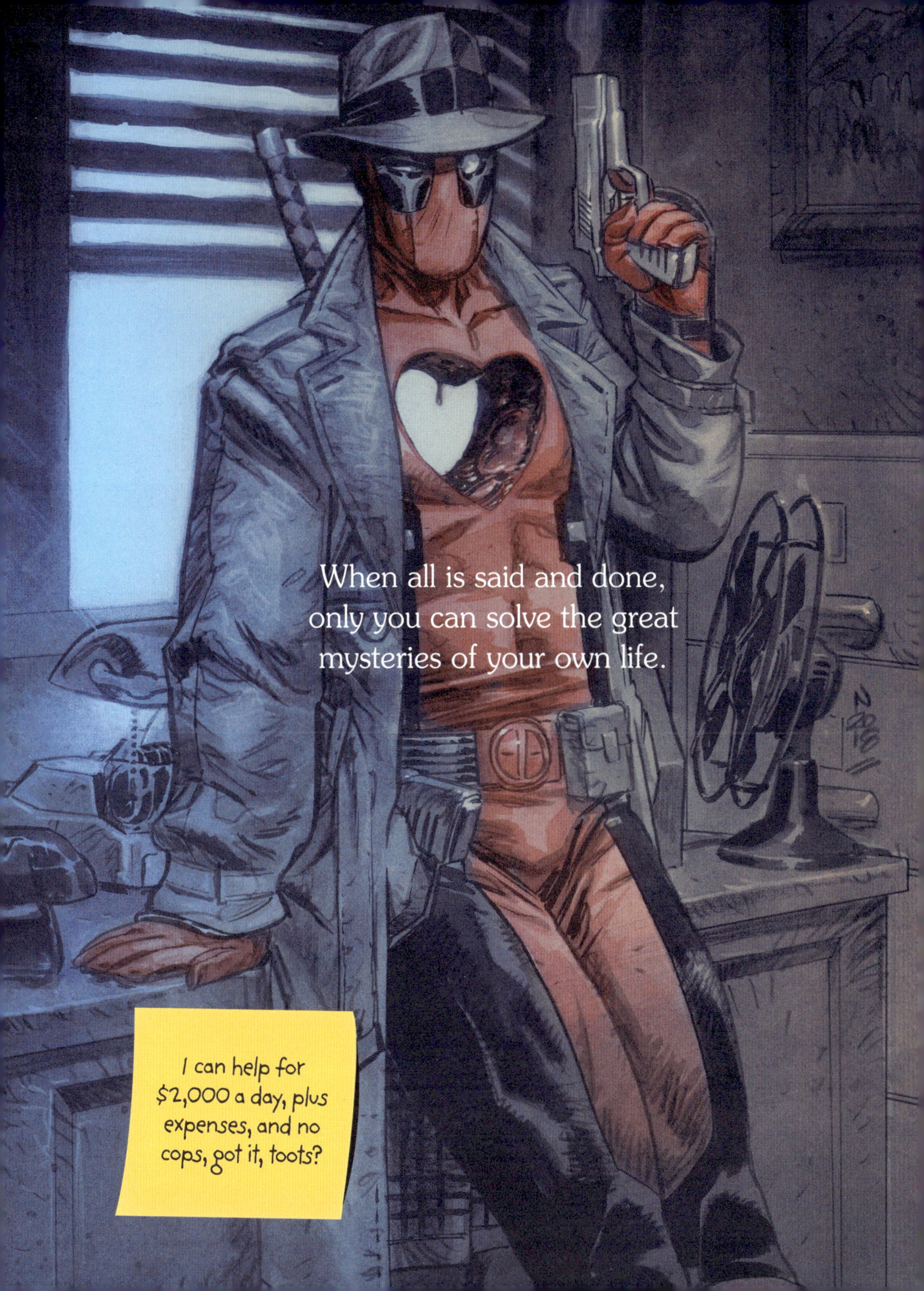
I can help for
$2,000 a day, plus
expenses, and no
cops, got it, toots?

When all is said and done, only you can solve the great mysteries of your own life.

You are enough—

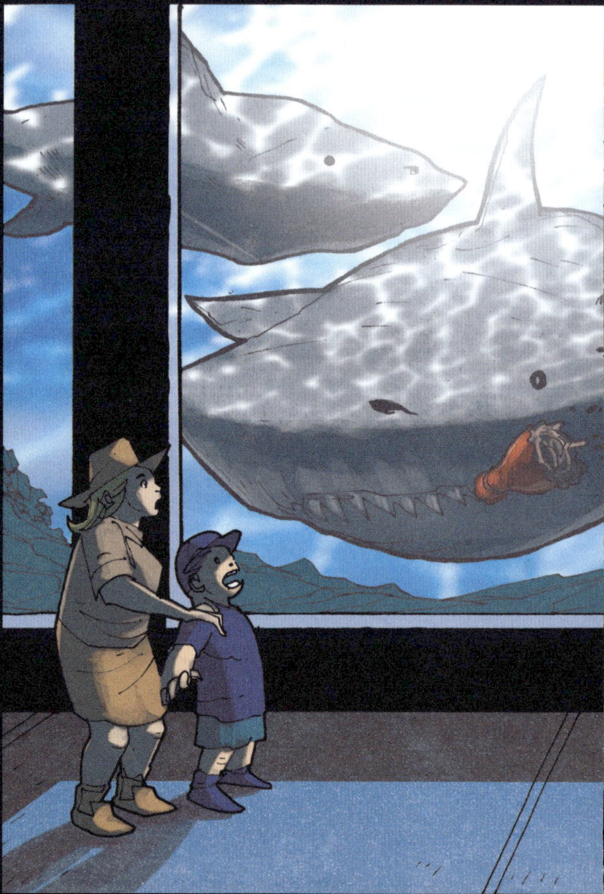

even when you're missing a few pieces.

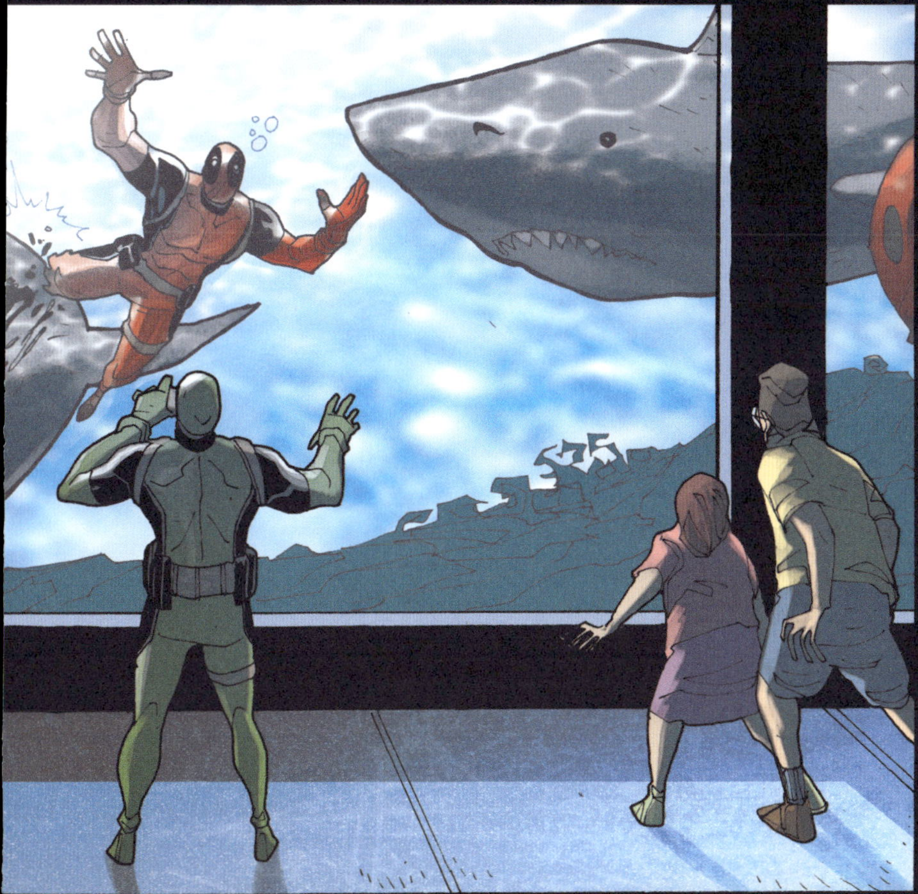

Let music fill you from head to toe,
until your heart and soul are full,
and your punches sing.

If you're waking up three
times a night to pee music,
yeah, that's probably too
much music. Dial it back.

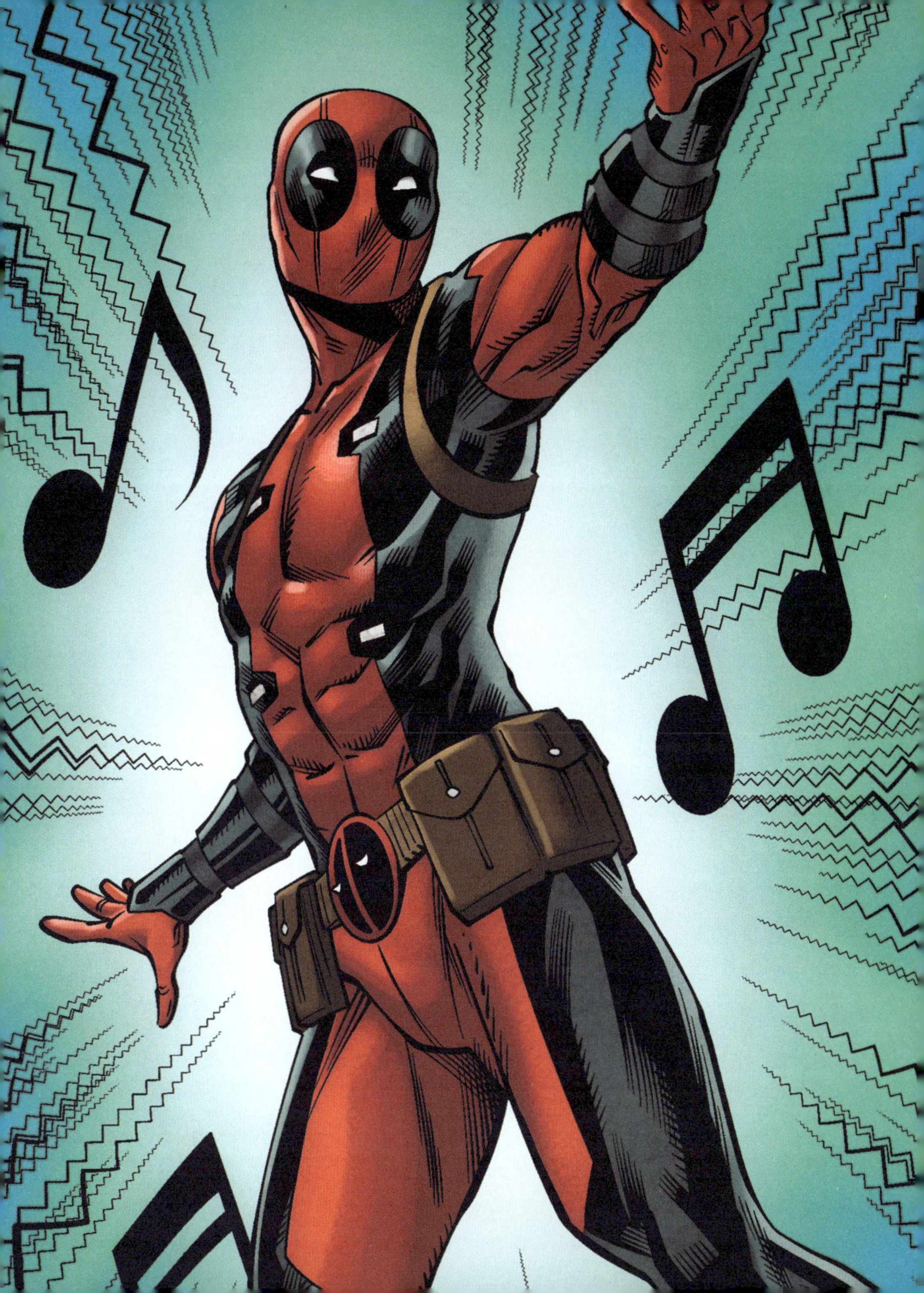

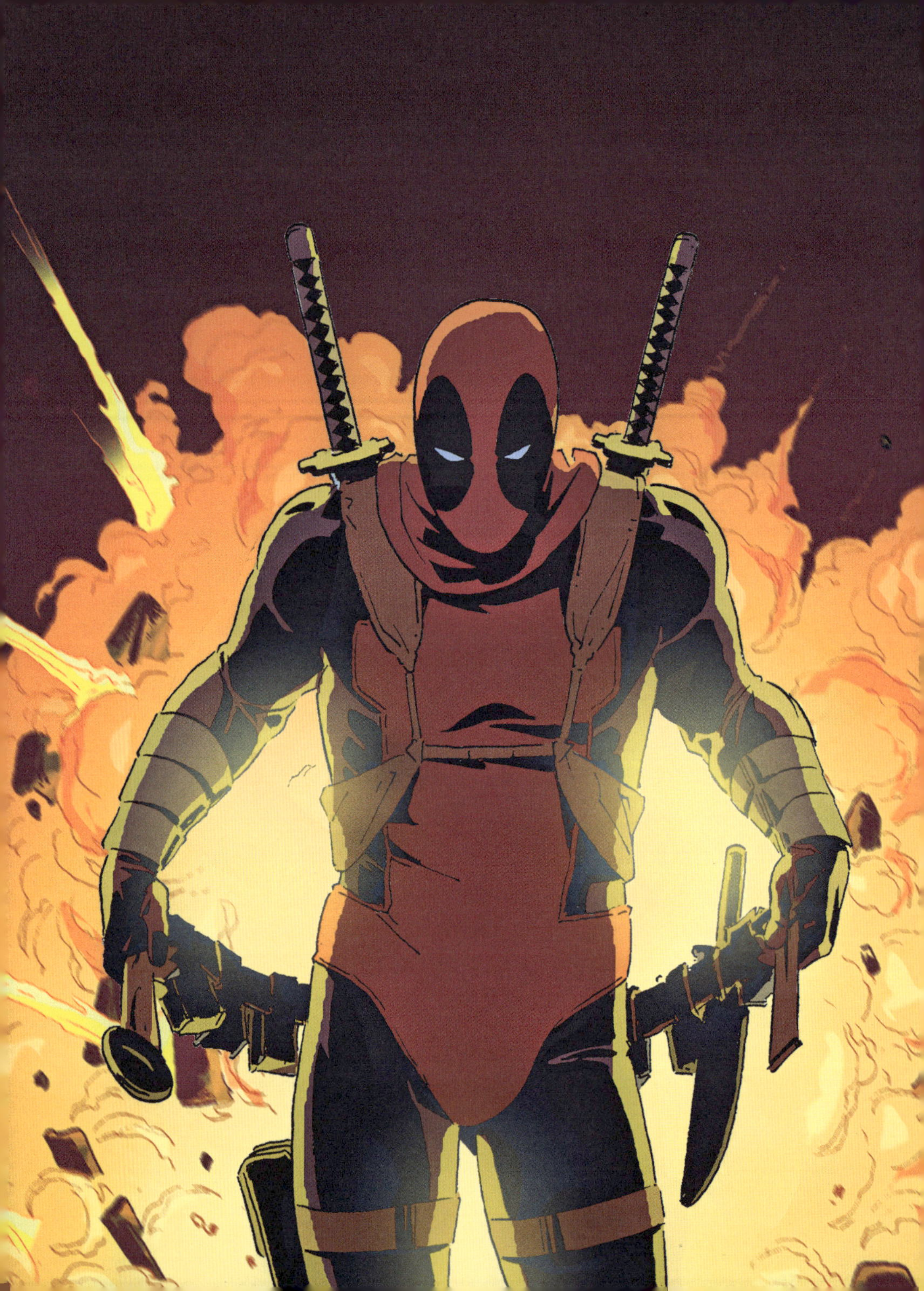

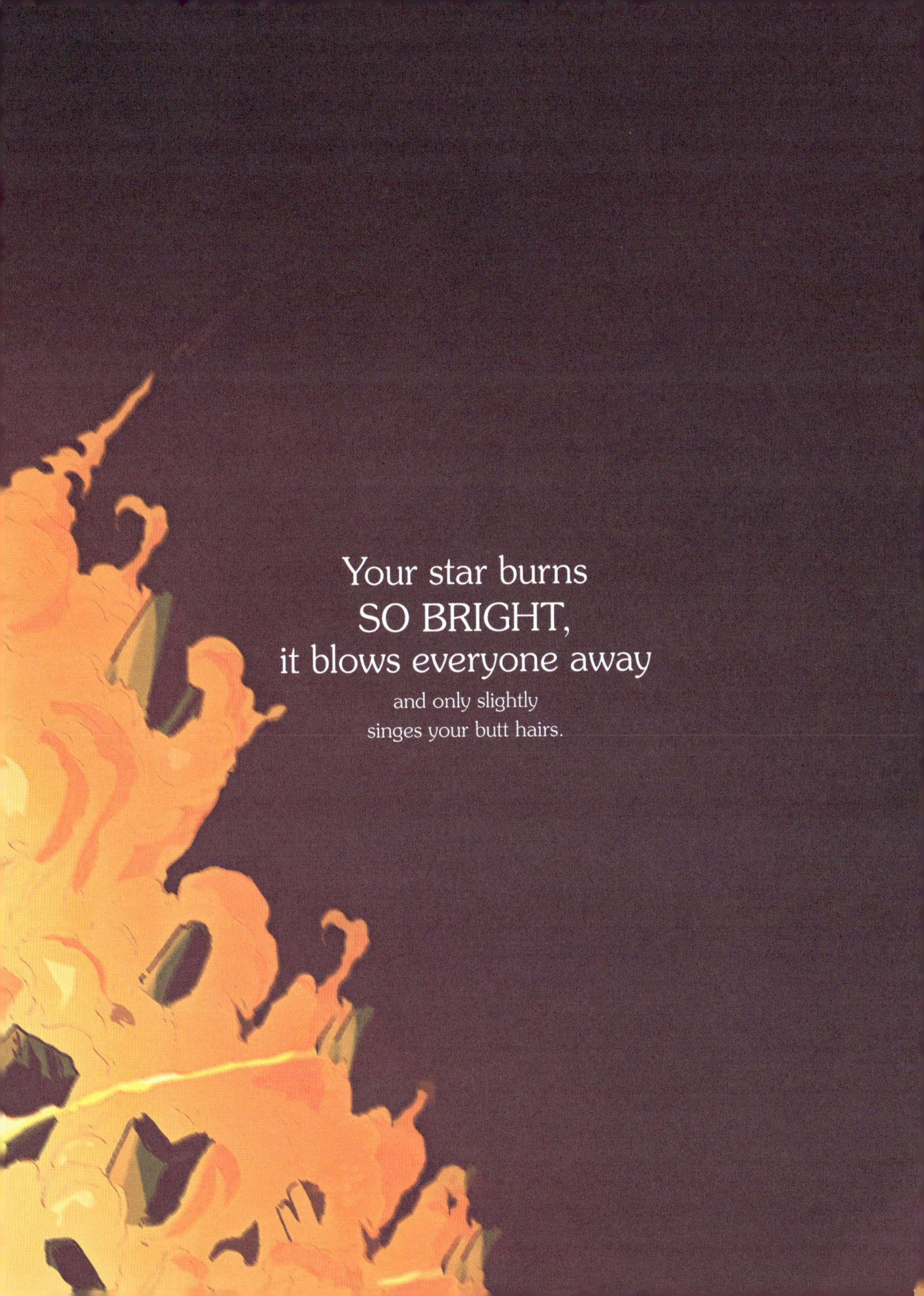
Your star burns
SO BRIGHT,
it blows everyone away
and only slightly
singes your butt hairs.

Take a big ol' bite out of life
like it's your cheat day!

PS: Calories don't count when you're
actively regenerating parts of yourself
(like your conscience and your dignity).

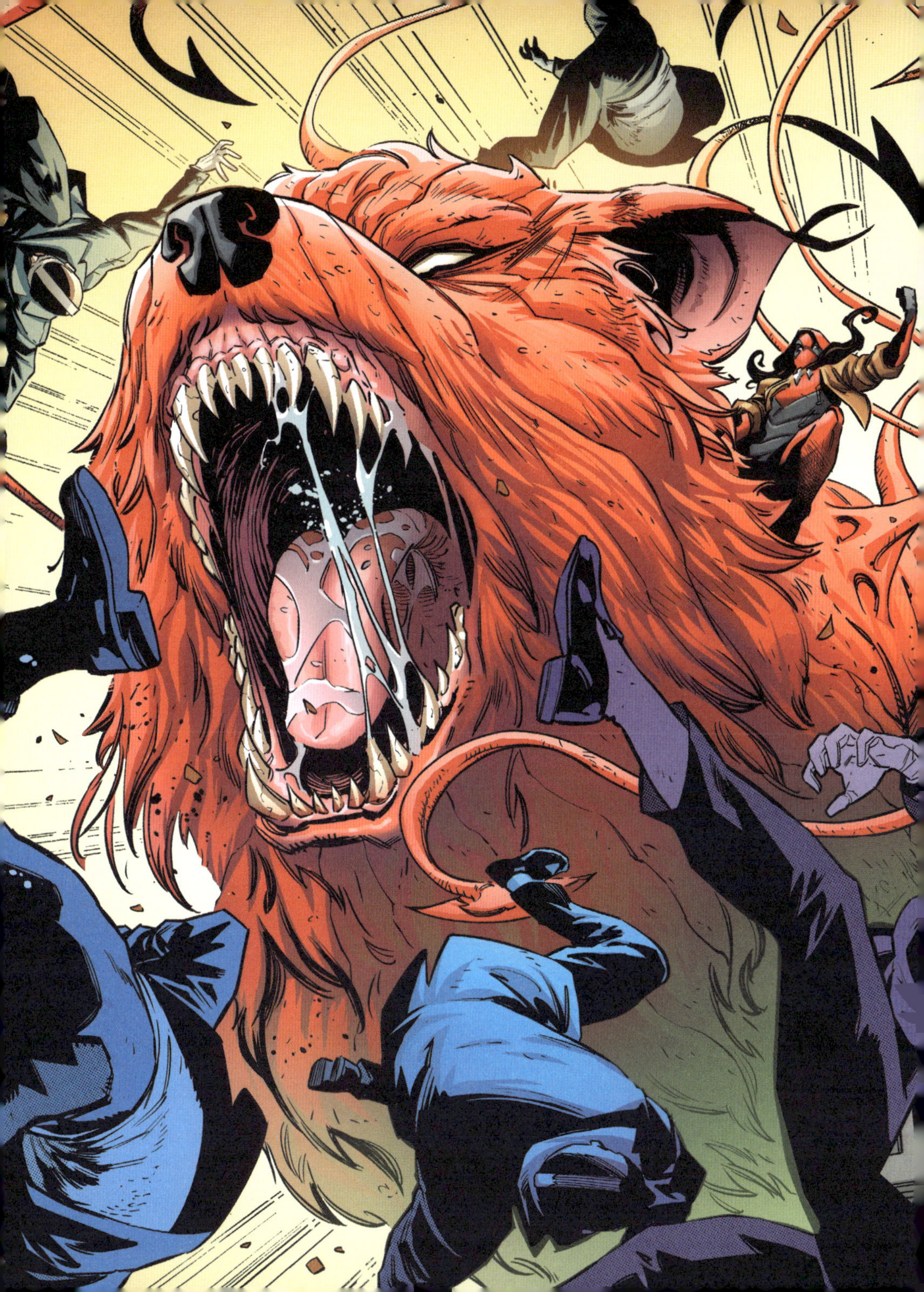

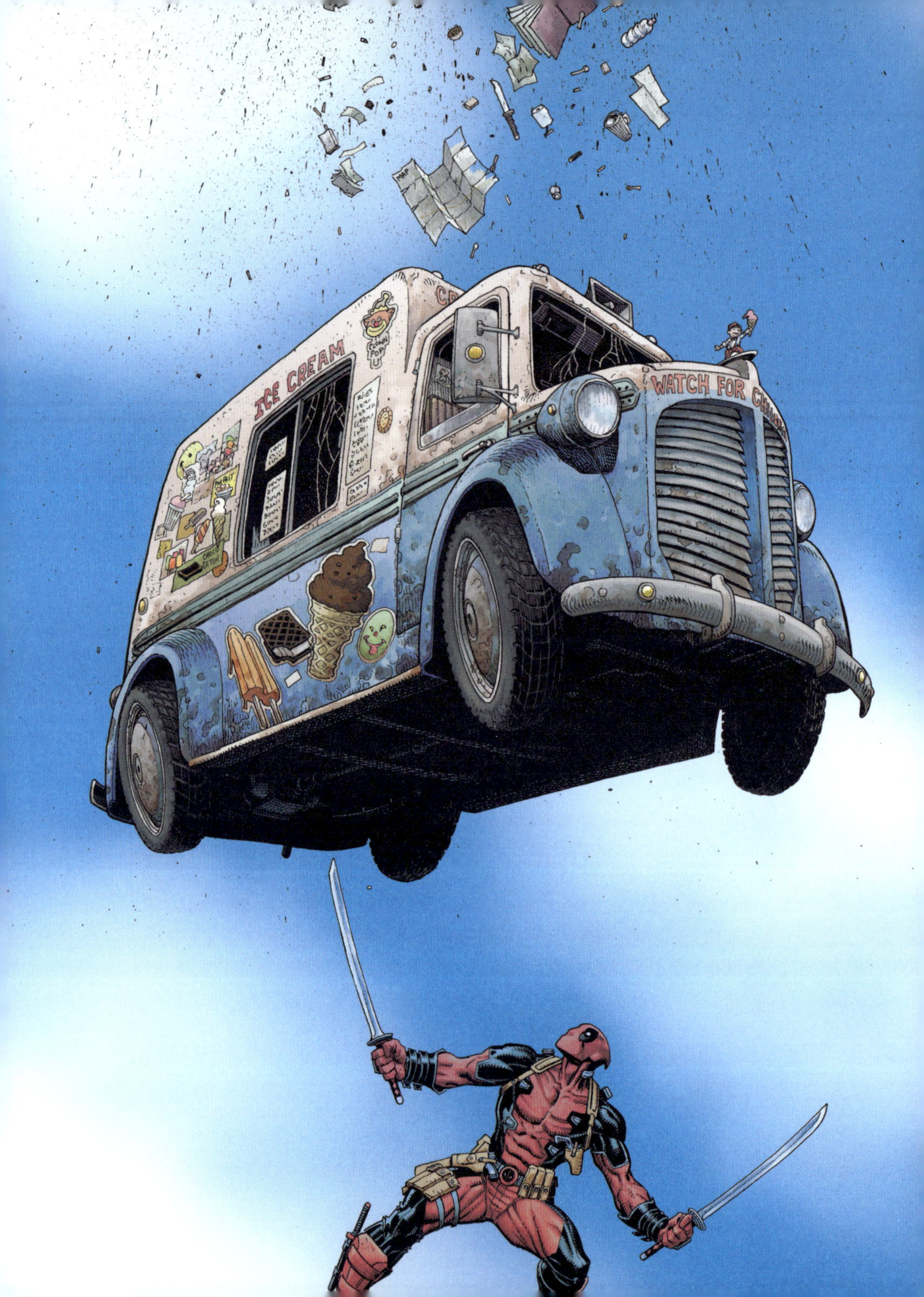
ICE CREAM
WATCH FOR

*Remember: At the end
of the day, you will always
get your just desserts.*

*Don't keep your
feelings bottled up.*

*They will burn through
your insides like that habanero
sauce you mistakenly
thought was the blood of your
enemies last night.*

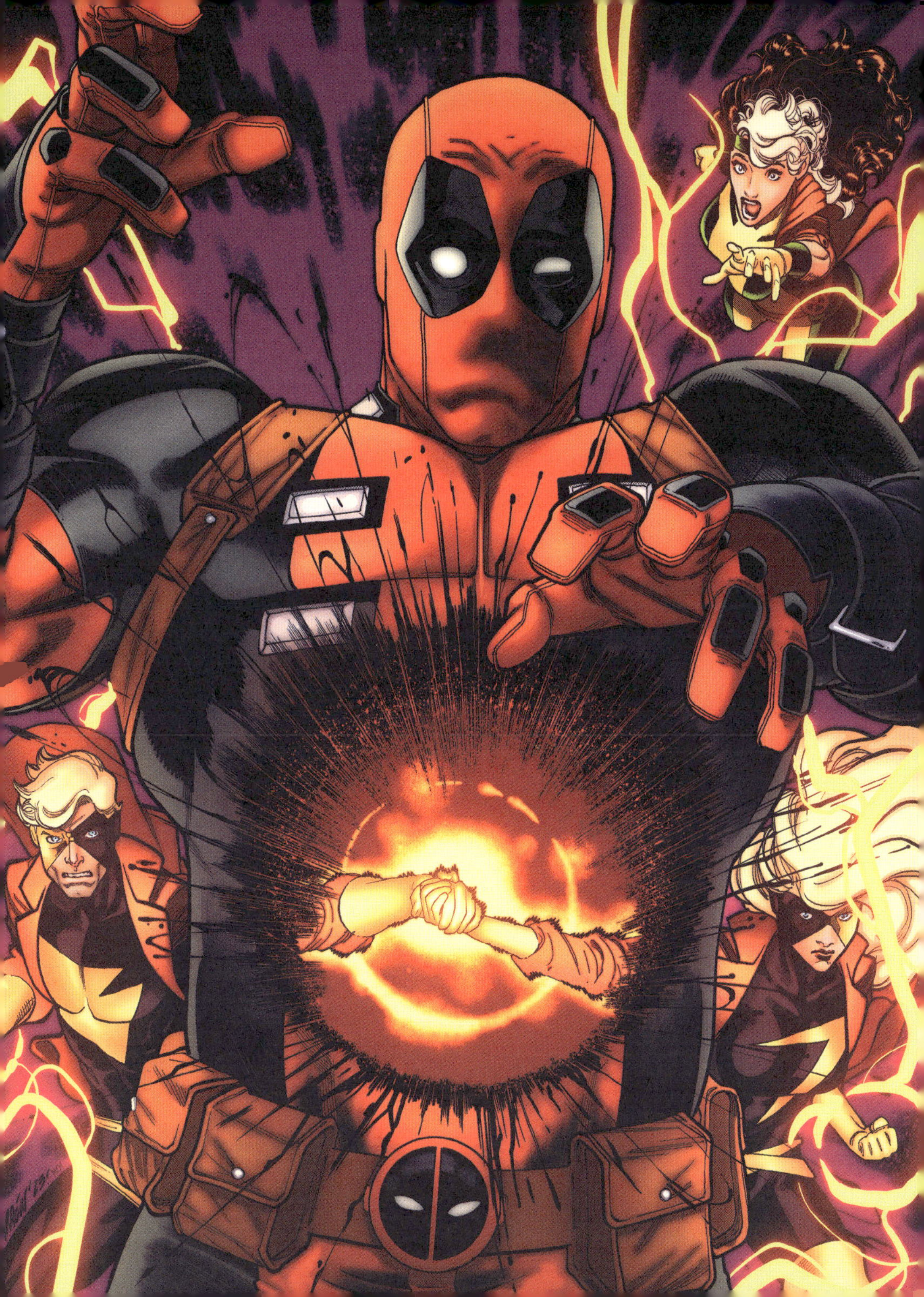

Practice gratitude every moment
of every day, until your neighbors
start banging on the walls, yelling,
"Enough with the gratitude
or we're calling the cops again!"

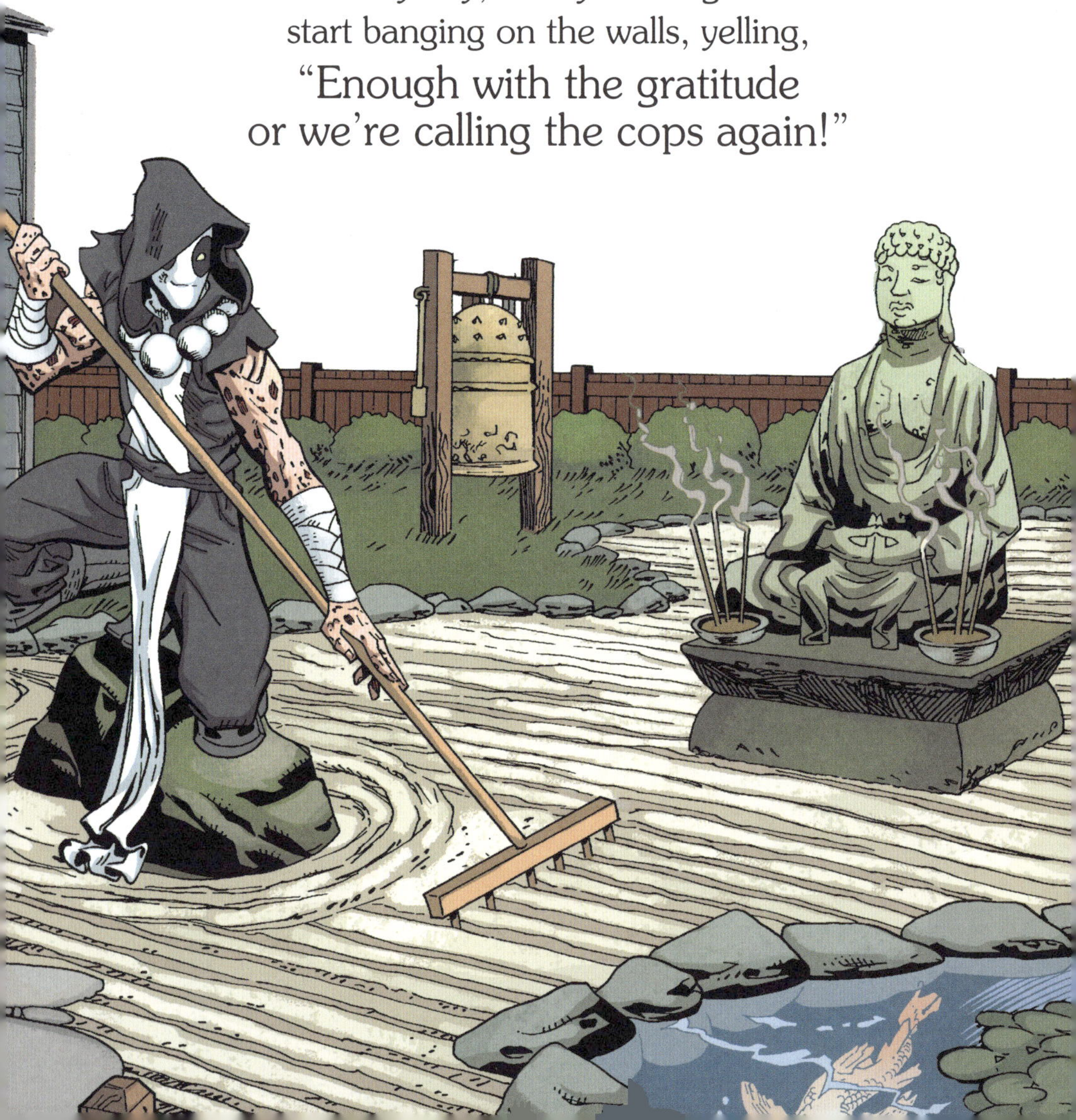

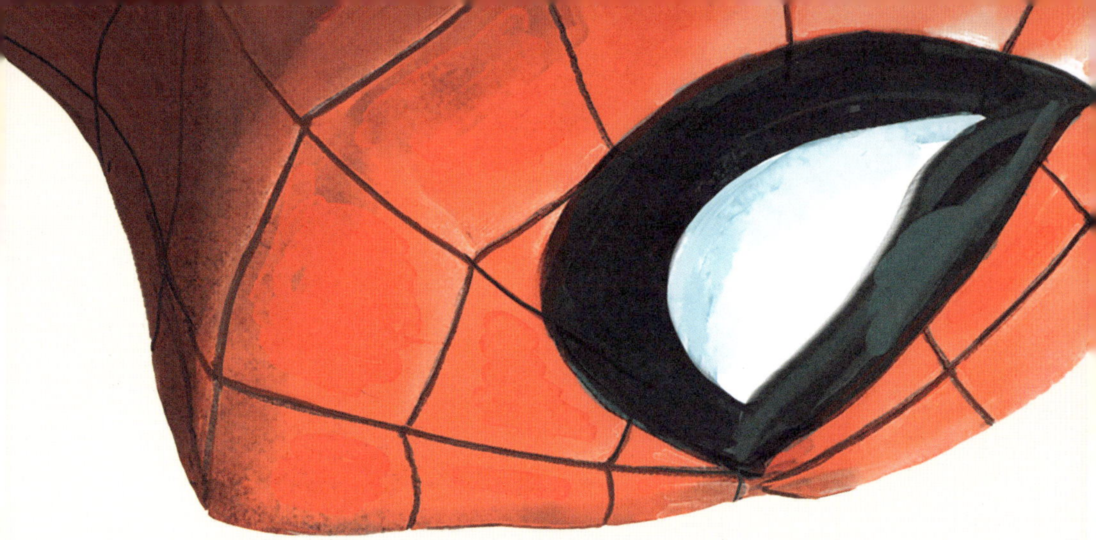

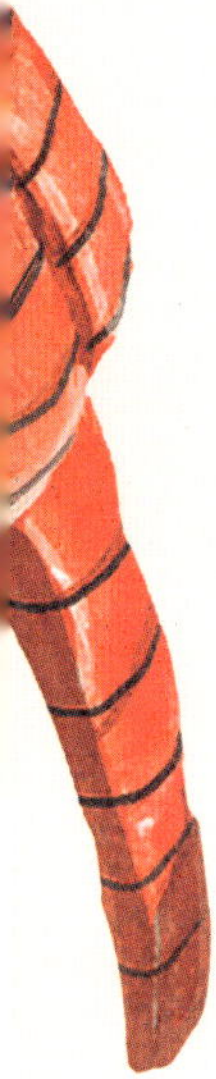

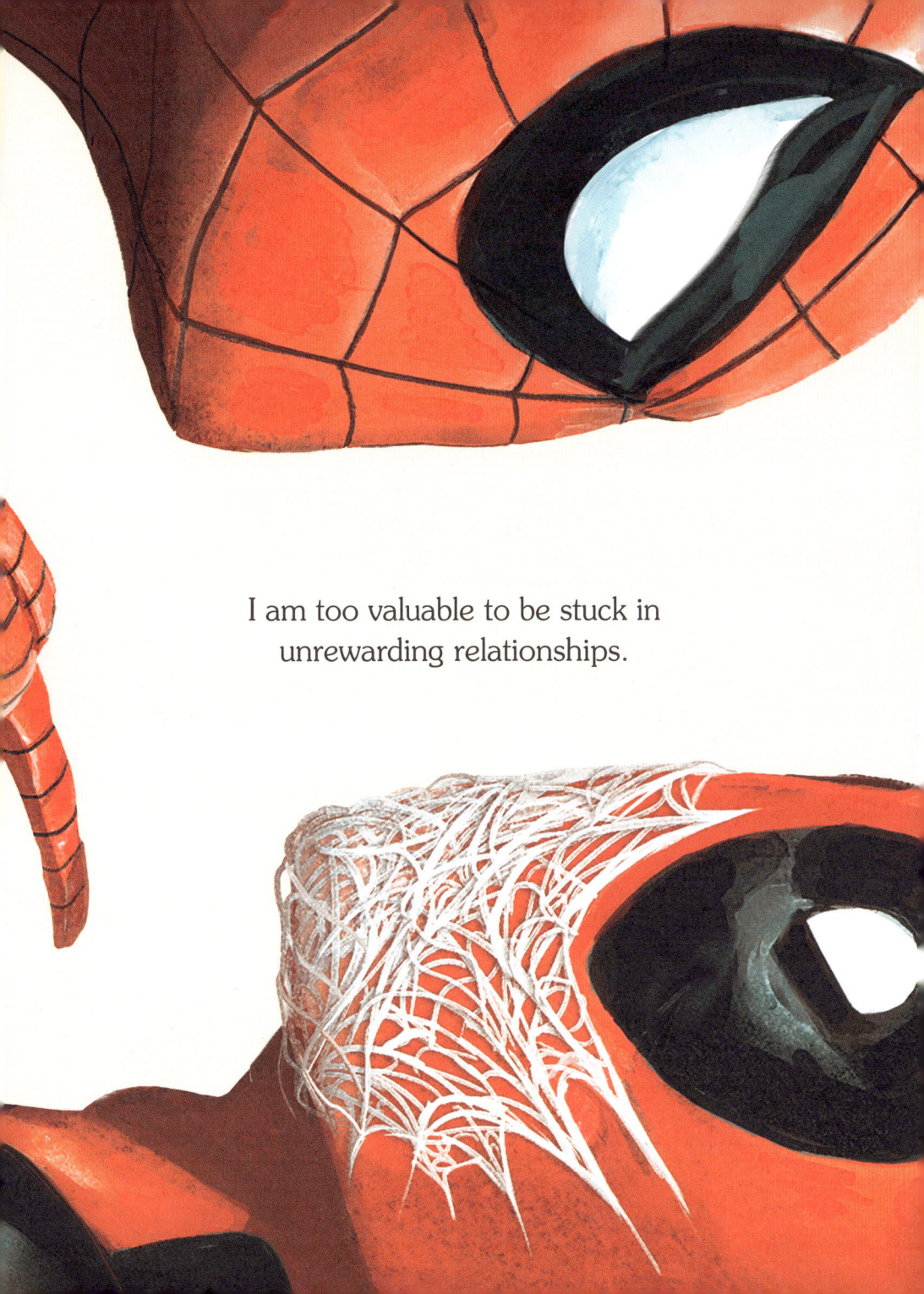

I am too valuable to be stuck in
unrewarding relationships.

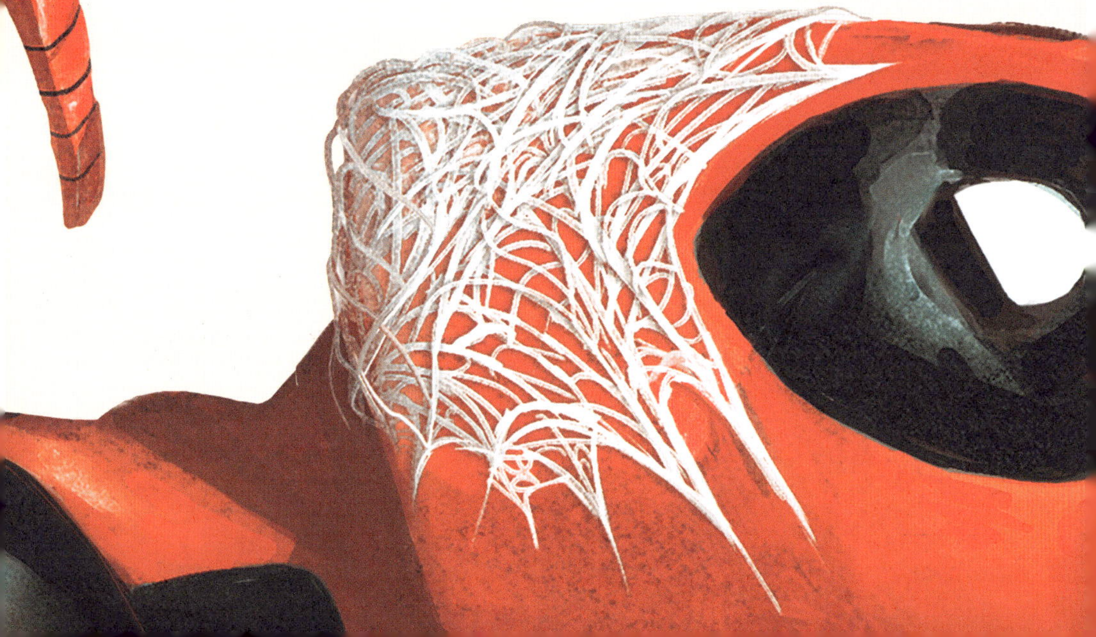

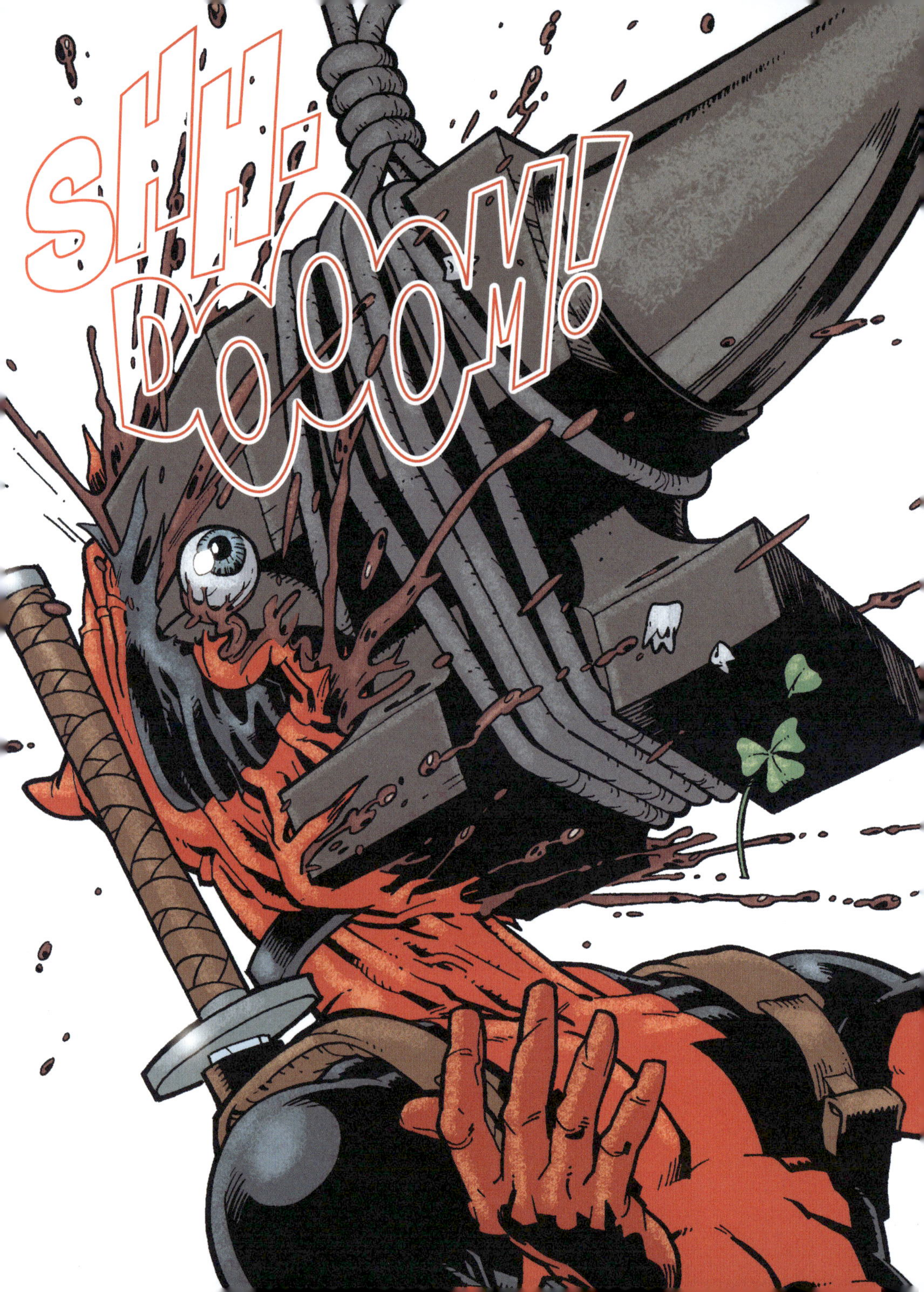
SHH-DOOOOM!

Don't be afraid to take a stand
and let the world know what you're
willing to fight and die

and fight and die

and fight and die

and fight and die

and fight and die

and fight and die

and fight and die

and fight and die

and fight and die

and fight and die

and fight and die

and fight and die

and fight and die for.

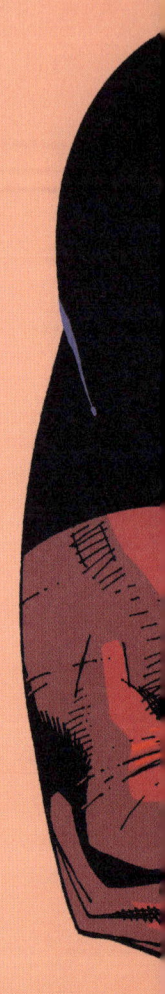

You're not lost.
You just occasionally
lose your head.

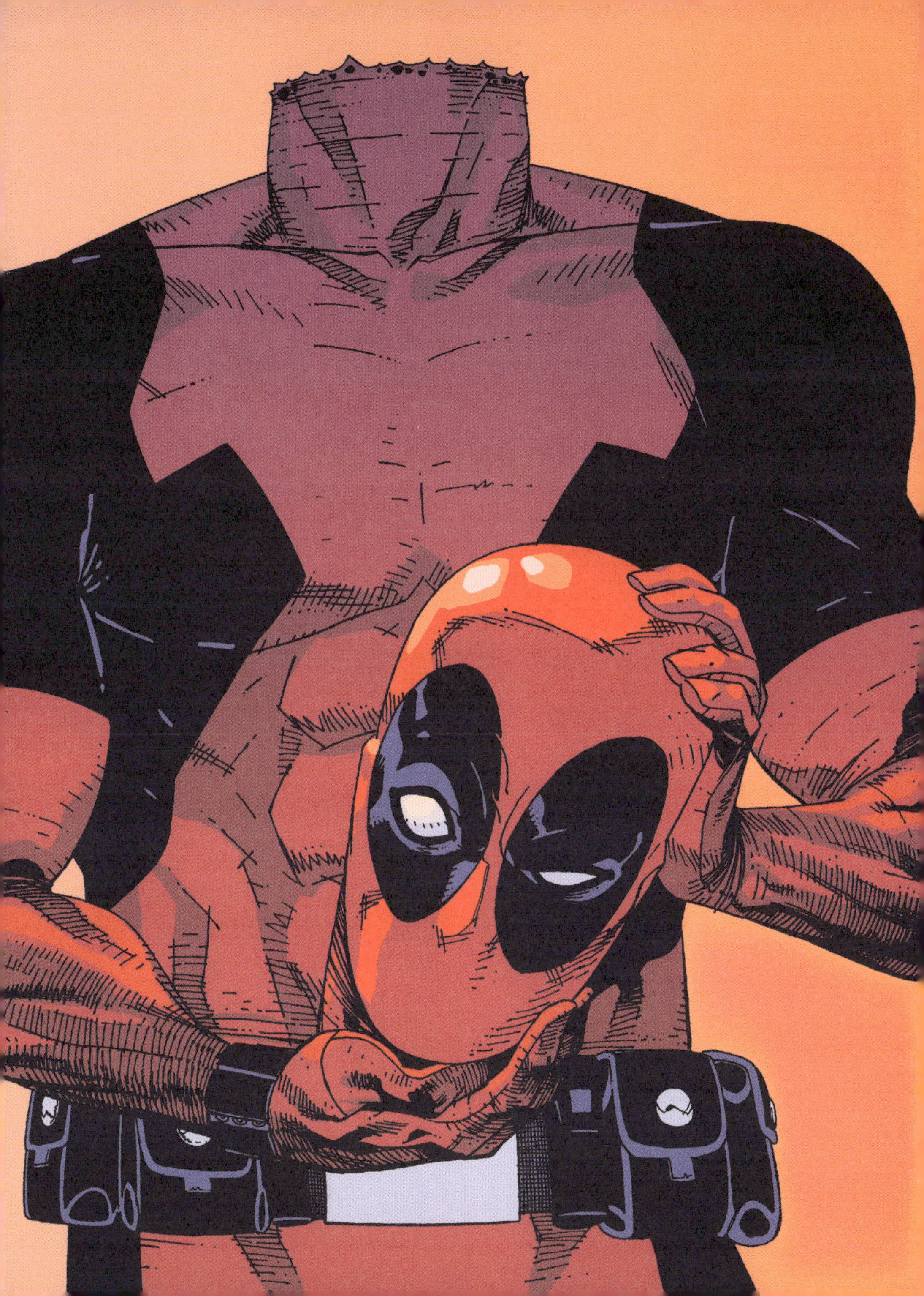

Believe me when
I say that it's never game over.

Even when it is game over.
Because you can always hit that
metaphorical start button again—or
steal someone else's game cartridge.

When all else fails,
remember your true super-power:
You look great in tights.

Guilt leaves you with a hole
that can only be filled by fresh
resolve, and/or a Laser &
Taser Fun-Pak from one of
S.H.I.E.L.D.'s clearance sales!

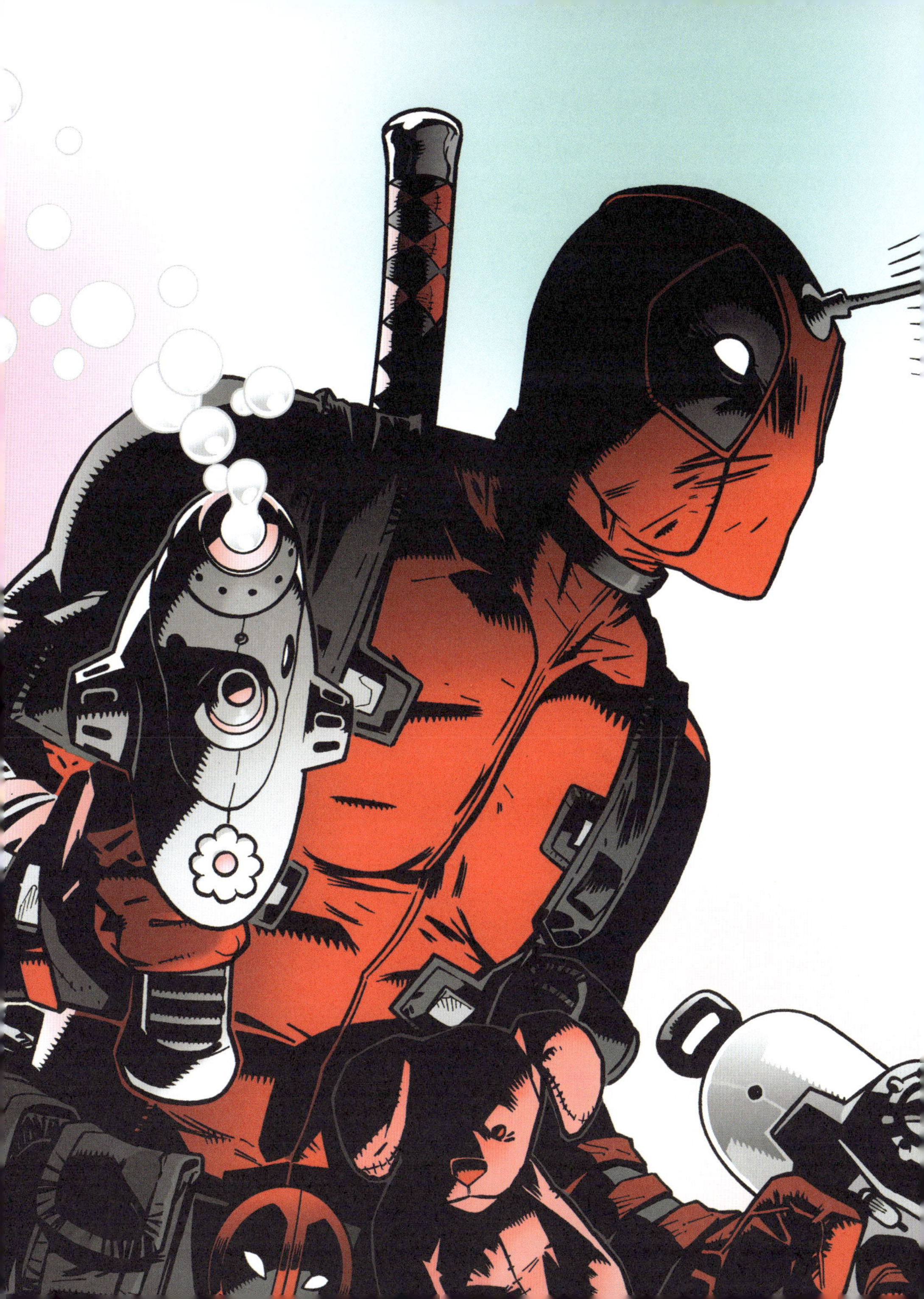

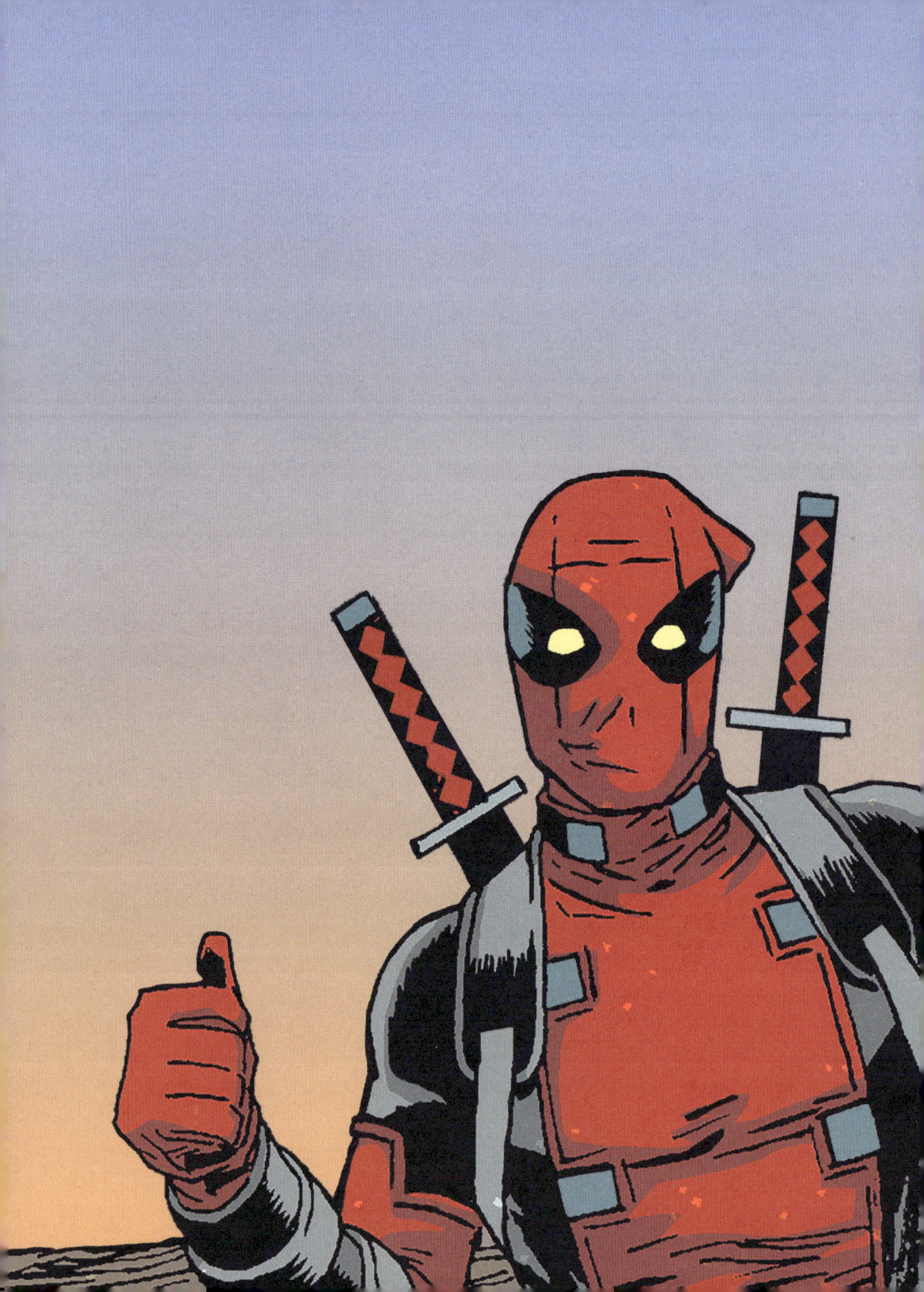

Brighten up someone's day
by leaving little surprise notes
that say "Thinking of you"
and "You're terrific!" and

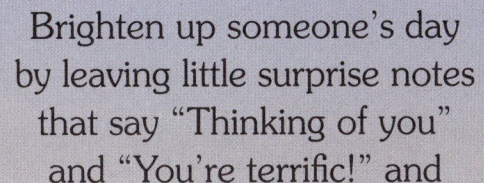

I'M SUUUPER
CONCERNED ABOUT
THAT MOLE
ON YOUR ▇▇▇▇

↖ THIS
SAYS ASS

Don't beat yourself up.

That's what Peanut is for.

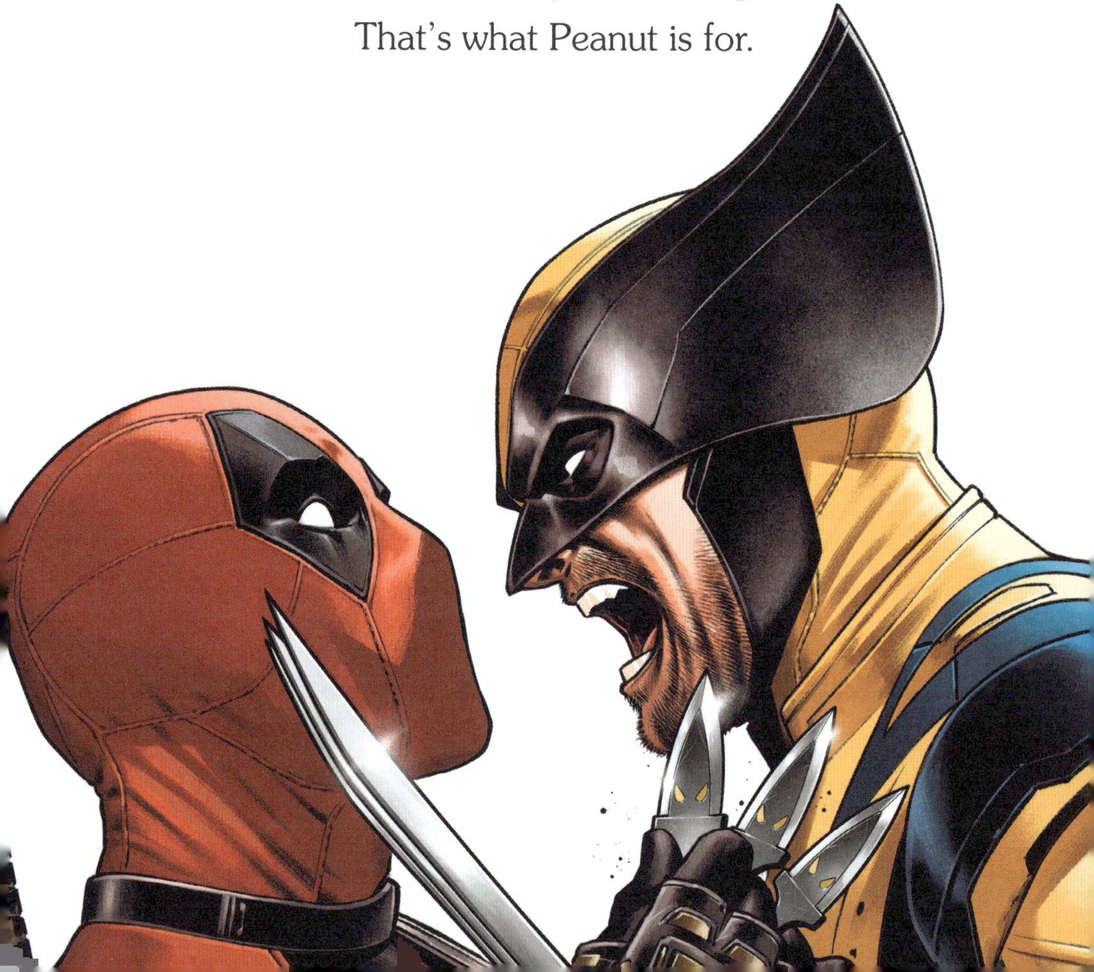

NEW
NICKNAME
ALERT:

Merc
with the
Moves!!!

Dance like everybody's watching,

and they are,

because you really are
the best dancer in the room.

The laughter of a child is the most powerful regenerative factor not created in a *$&#ed-up Canadian weapons lab.

PULL-MY-
FINGER JOKES
NEVER FAIL.
XO, DADPOOL

Sometimes the friend you
need most is right there under your
nose. Waiting to help . . .
or to run off with your fibula.

*Surround yourself
with people who see who
you really are inside.*

*Or people who'll help
you find your insides.
Either is good.*

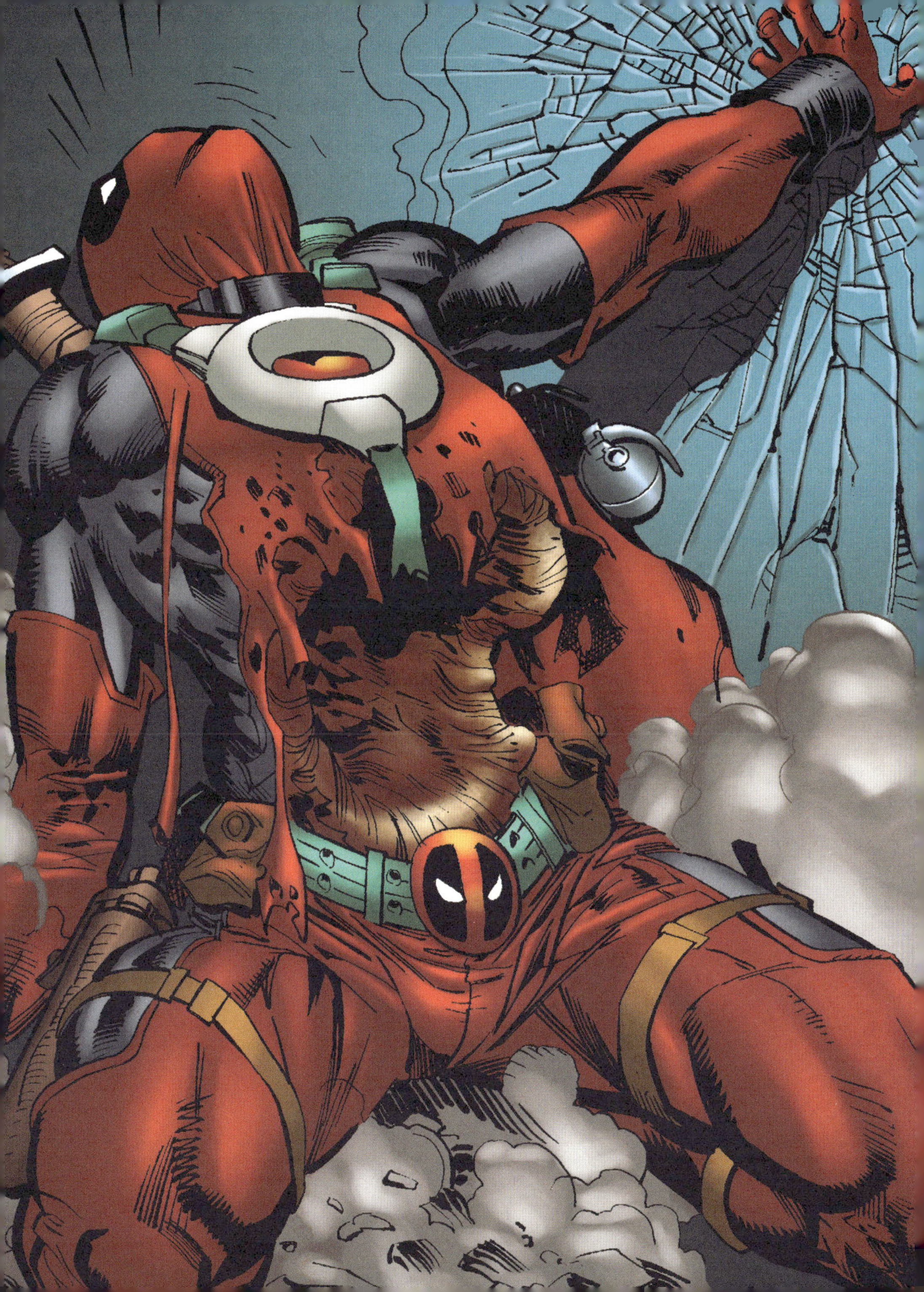

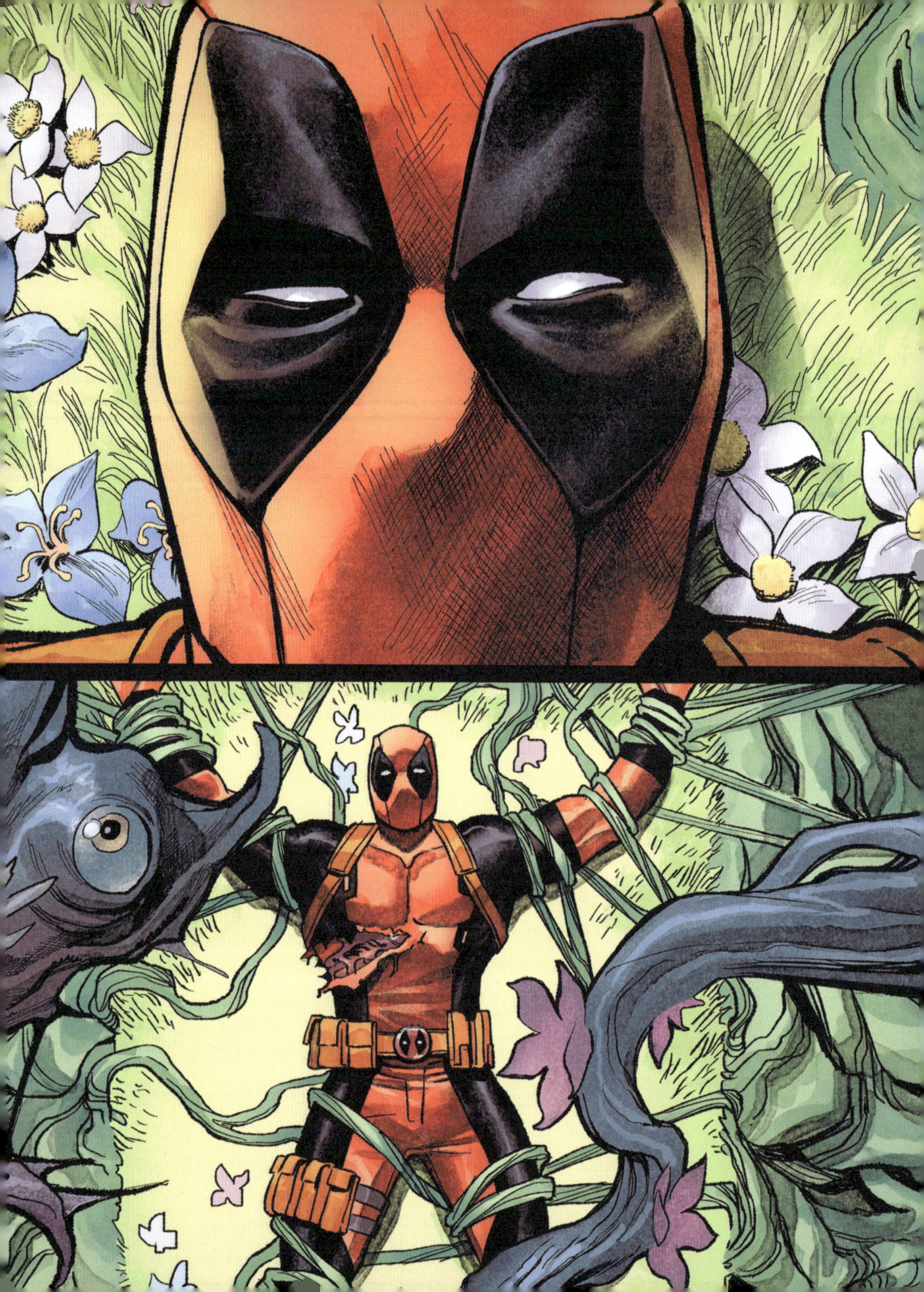

Imagine yourself in a
peaceful, meditative place in nature
and breathe deep.
Ignore the vines "hugging" your legs.

HELP YOURSELF

You have all the ~~self-help~~ tools
you need to turn this day around:
breathing exercises, a lavender
diffuser, swords, chainsaws …

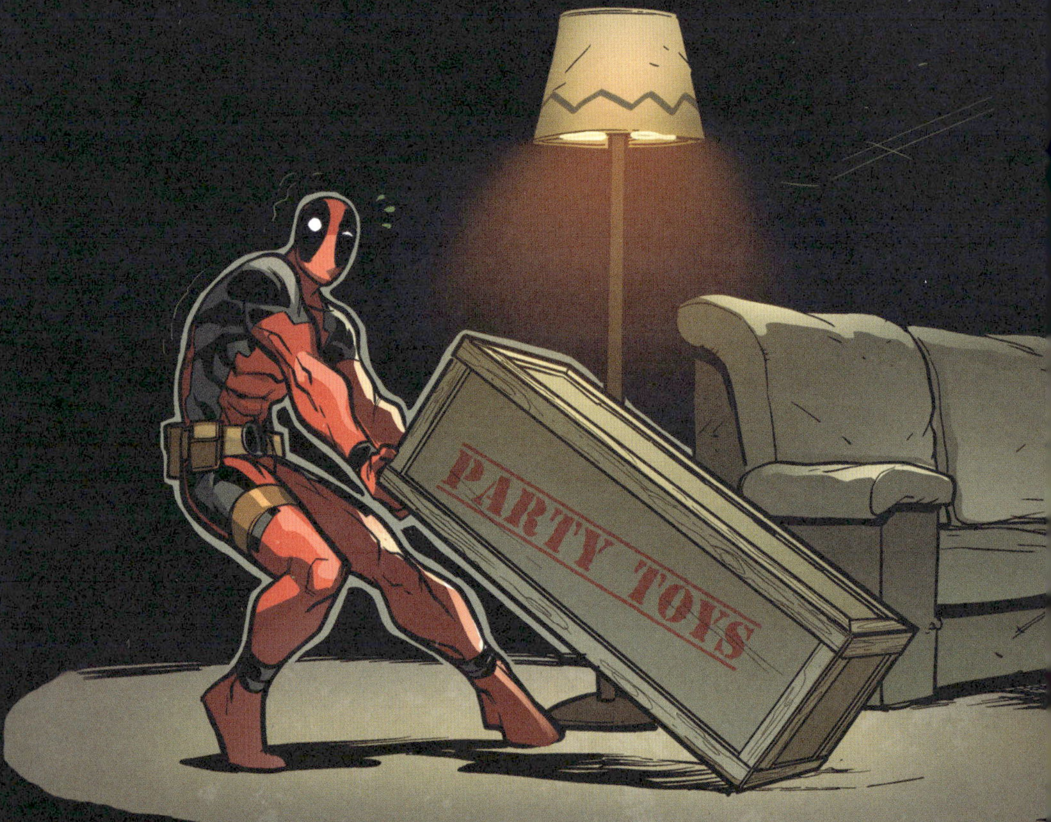
PARTY TOYS

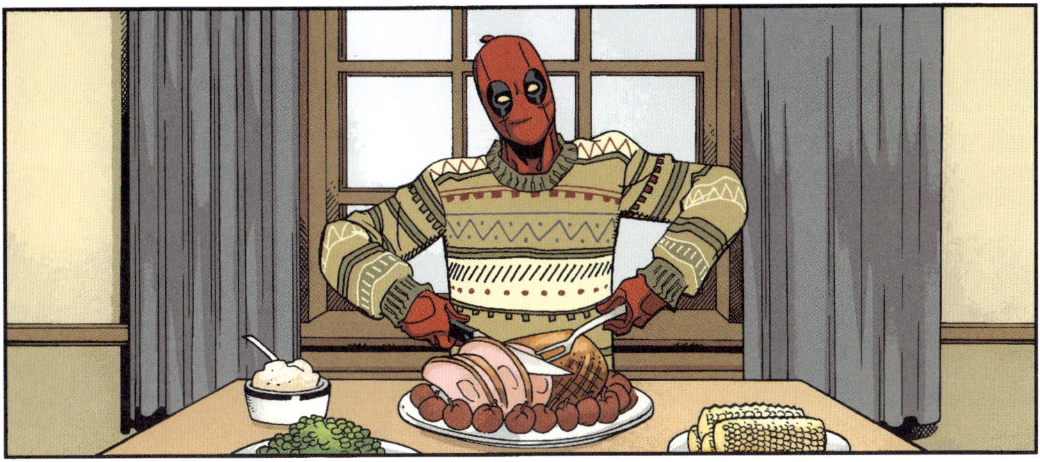

All together now:

Dress the part!
Act the part!
Lose the parts!
Grow the parts!

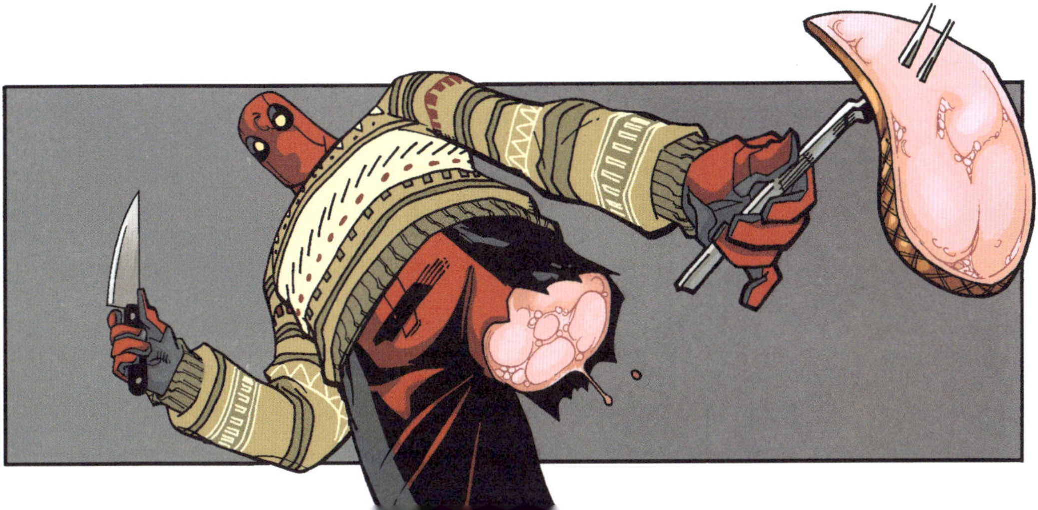

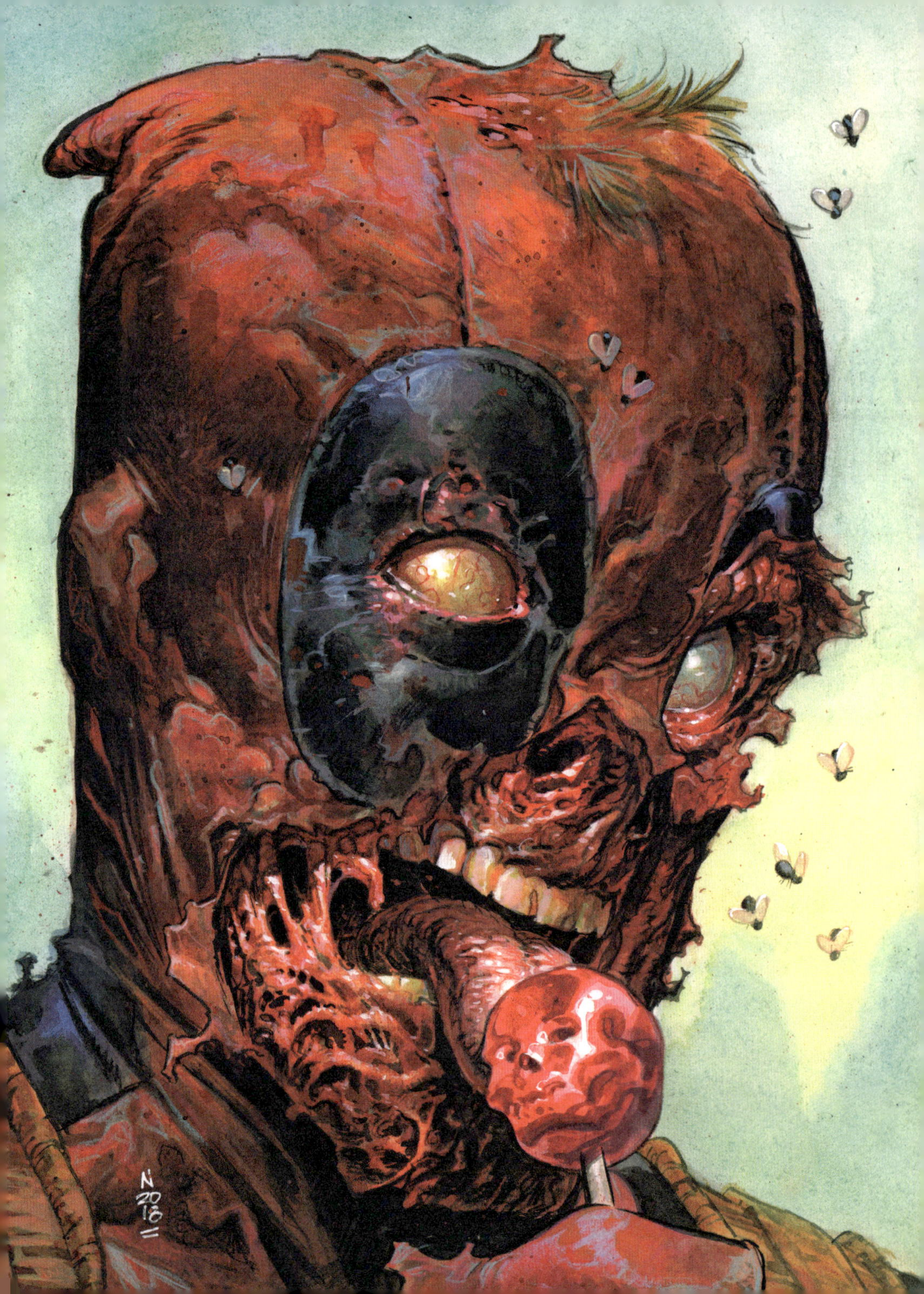

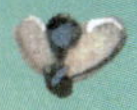

You've got
what it takes!

Yes, you. Over there.

Sorry, my eye is
still un-charbroiling.

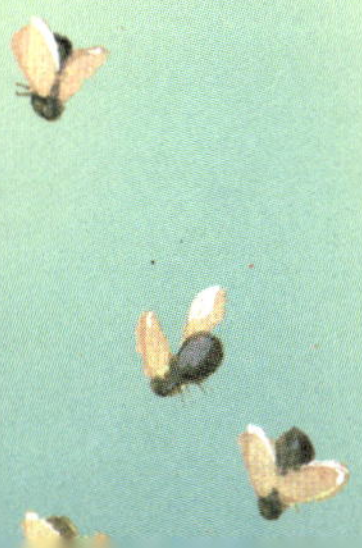

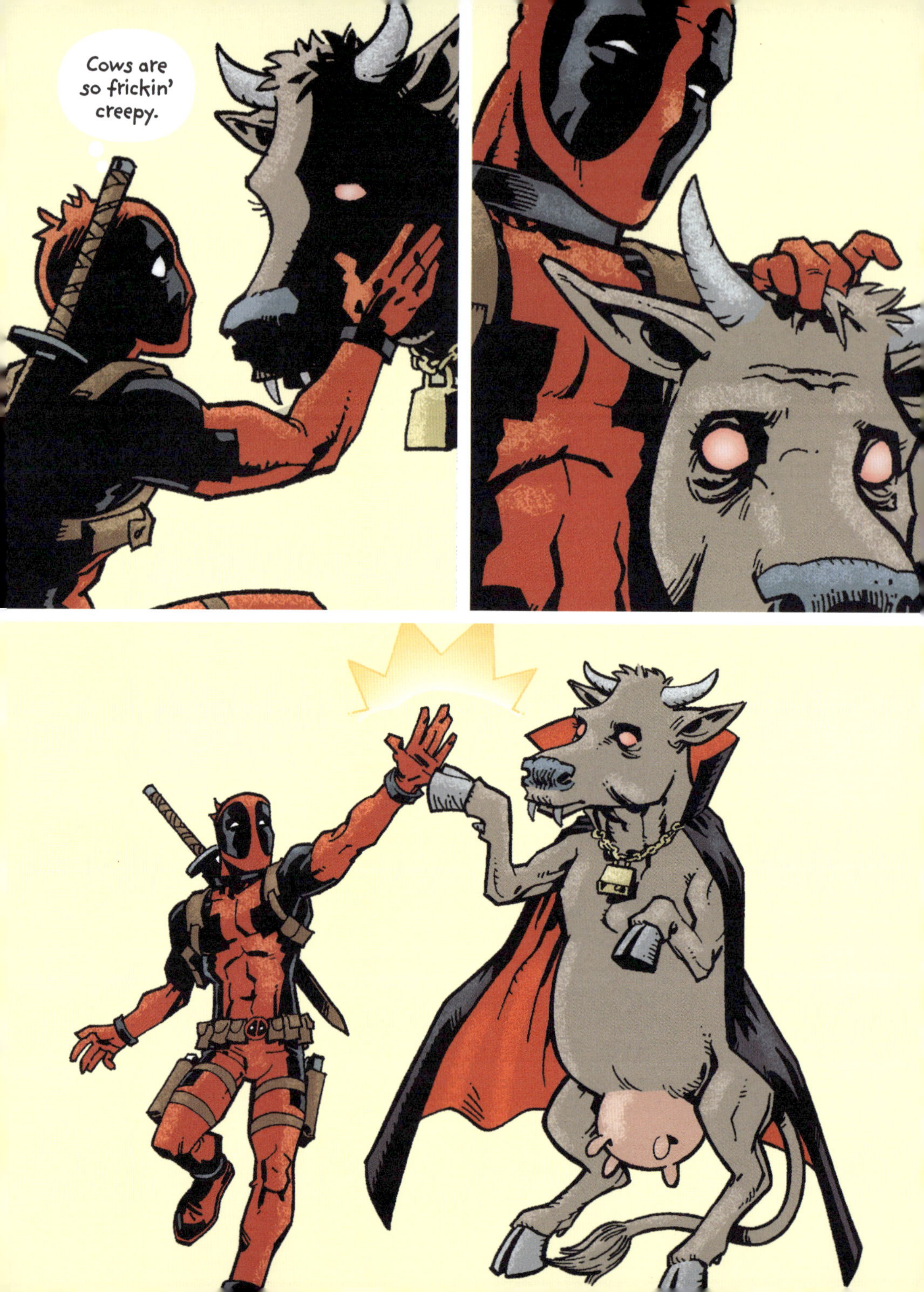
Cows are so frickin' creepy.

I am stronger than my fears.
I am stronger than my fears.
I am stronger than my fears.
I am stronger than my fears.
I am stronger than my fears.
I am stronger than my fears.
I am stronger than my fears.

Believe in yourself,

and your ability
to cause maximum mayhem.

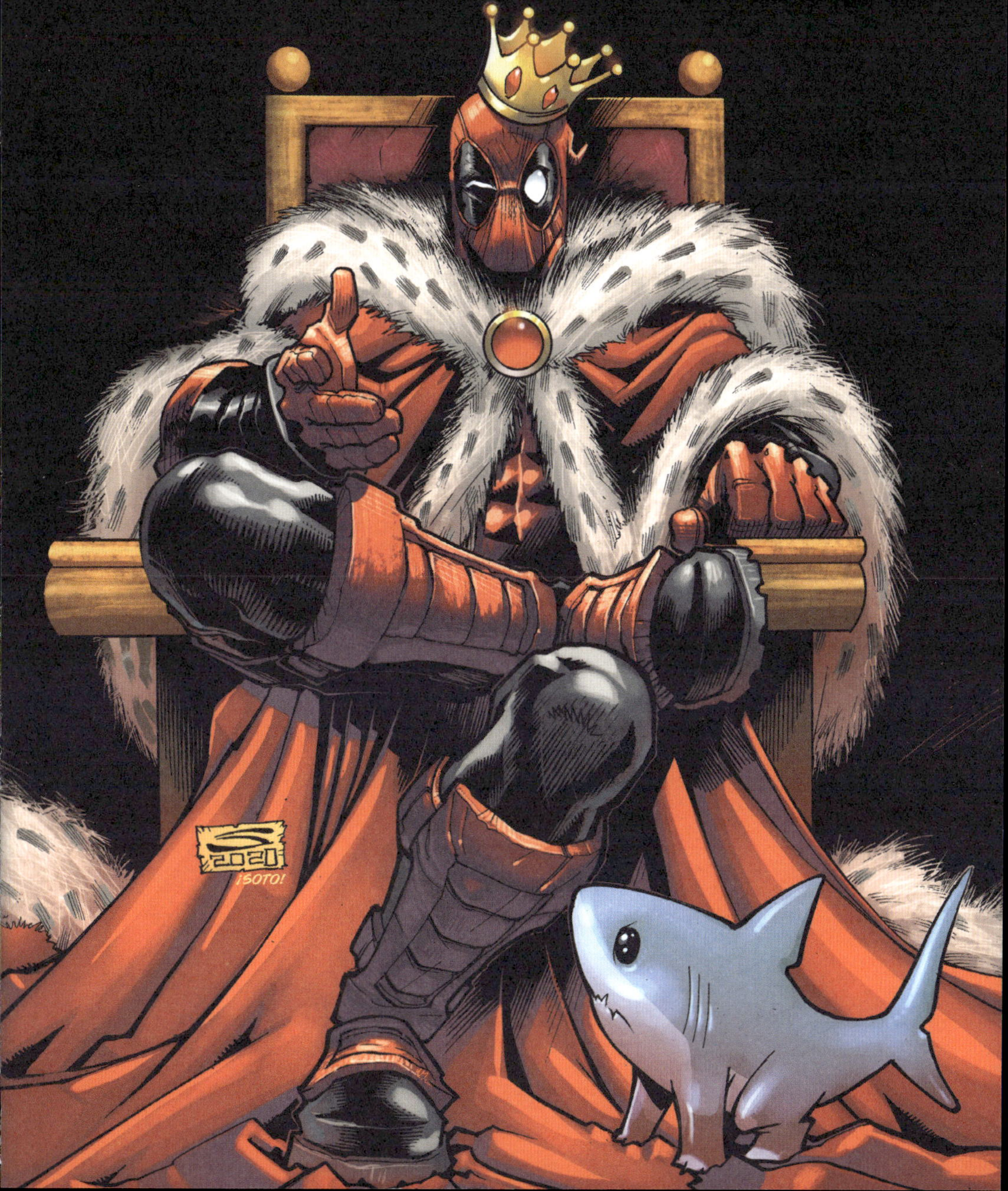
2020
¡SOTO!

Random House Worlds
An imprint of Random House
A division of Penguin Random House LLC
1745 Broadway, New York, NY 10019
randomhousebooks.com
penguinrandomhouse.com

Hardcover ISBN 978-0-593-98481-9

Ebook ISBN 978-0-593-98482-6

Printed in China on acid-free paper

2 4 6 8 9 7 5 3 1

First Edition

MARVEL BOOK TEAM:
Jeff Youngquist, VP, Production and Special Projects
Brian Overton, Manager, Special Projects
Sarah Singer, Editor, Special Projects
Jeremy West, Manager, Licensed Publishing
Sven Larsen, VP, Licensed Publishing
David Gabriel, VP, Print & Digital Publishing
C. B. Cebulski, Editor in Chief

RHW BOOK TEAM:
Jacinta O'Halloran, Editor
Tomi Tunrarebi, Editorial Assistant
Walter Green, Designer
Susan Seeman, Managing Editor
Robert Siek, Production Editor
Erich Schoeneweiss, Production Manager

Cover photograph by Galyna Andrushko/Shutterstock | Cover design by Walter Green

The authorized representative in the EU for product safety and compliance is Penguin Random House Ireland, Morrison Chambers, 32 Nassau Street, Dublin D02 YH68, Ireland. https://eu-contact.penguin.ie

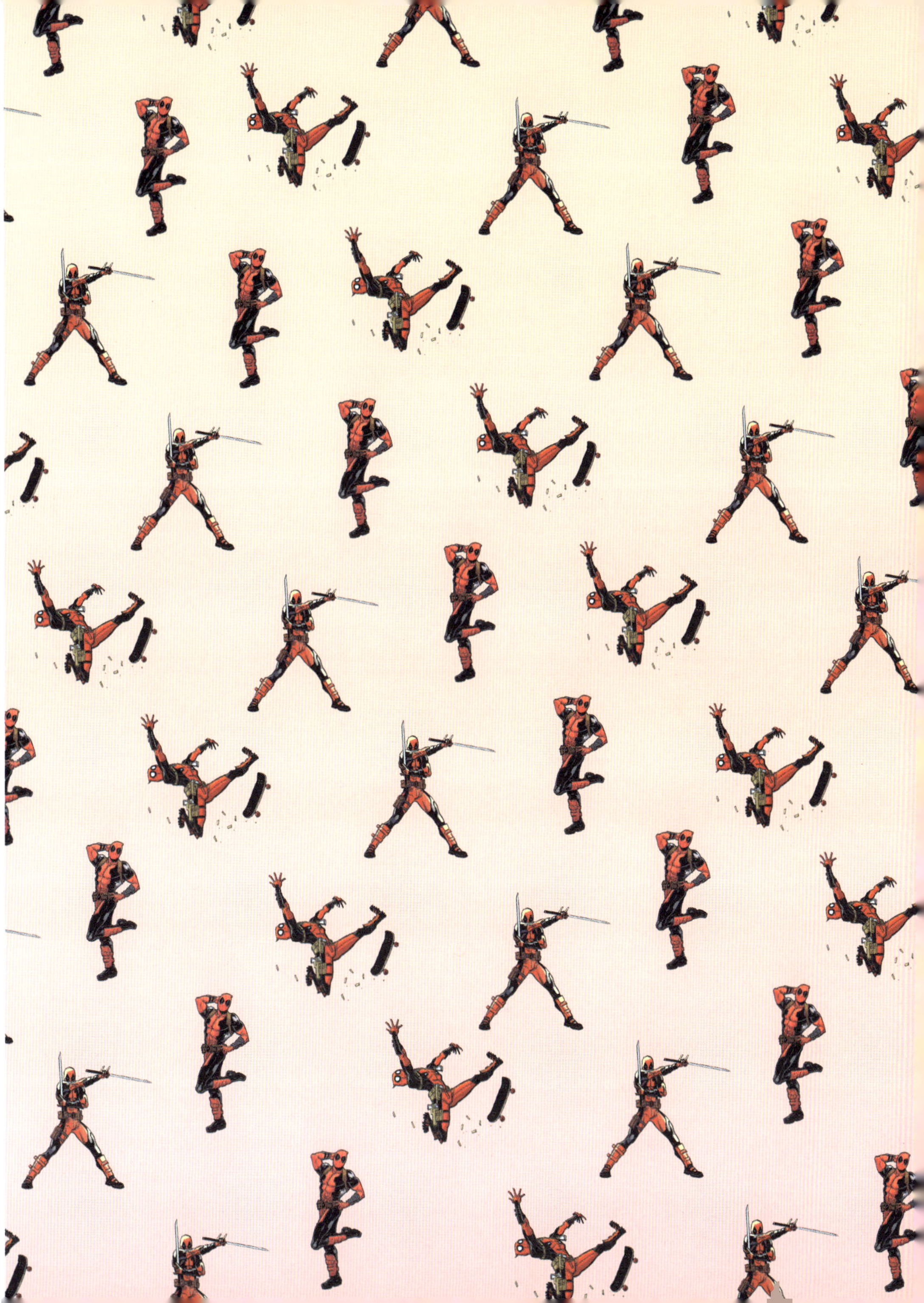

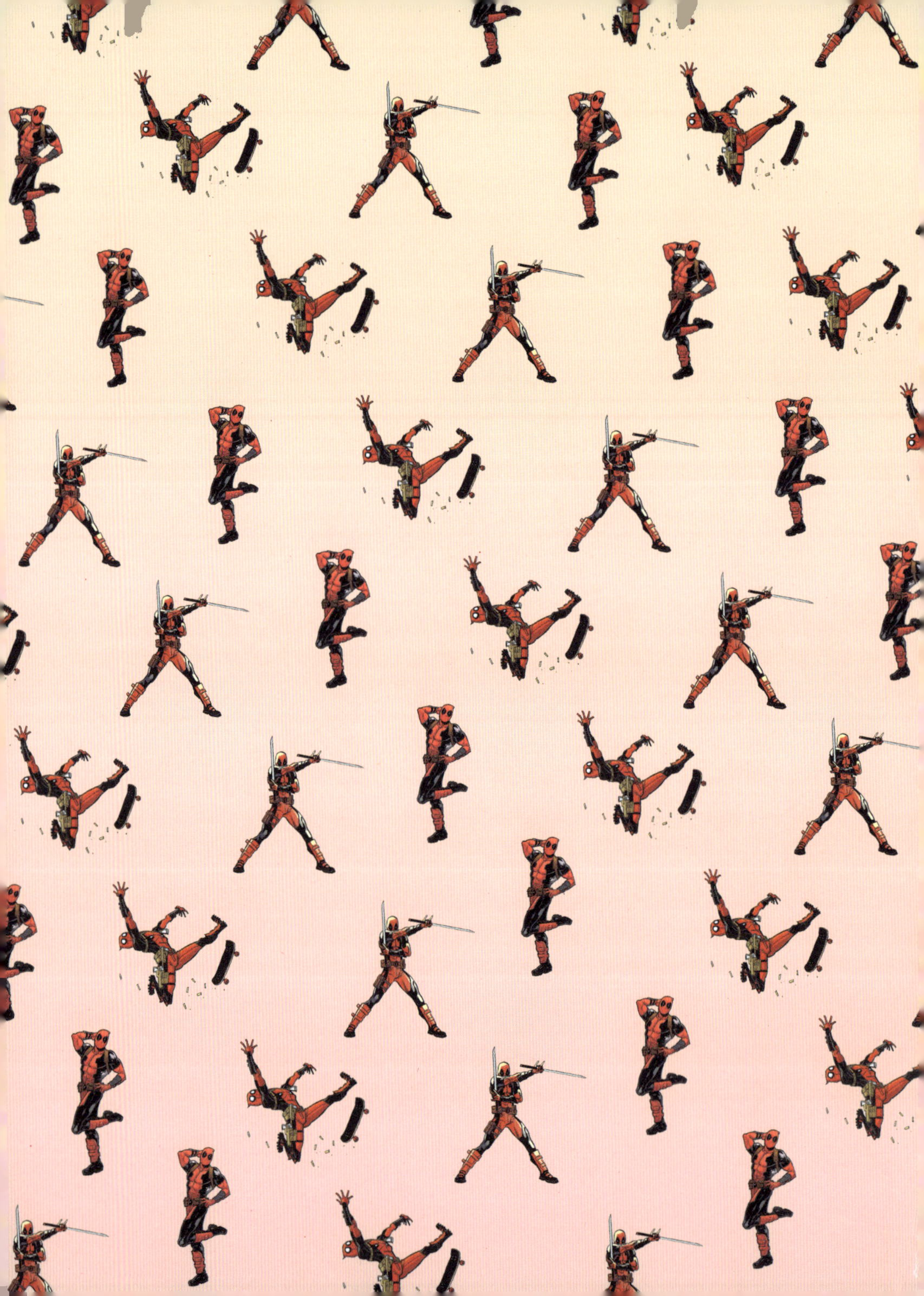